CHILDHOOD

Edited by C

First published in Great Britain in 2015 by

Policy Press
University of Bristol
1-9 Old Park Hill
Bristol
BS2 8BB
UK
t: +44 (0)117 954 5940
pp-info@bristol.ac.uk
www.policypress.co.uk

North America office:
Policy Press
c/o The University of Chicago Press
1427 East 60th Street
Chicago, IL 60637, USA
t: +1 773 702 7700
f: +1 773-702-9756
sales@press.uchicago.edu
www.press.uchicago.edu

ISBN 978-1-4473-2194-1 Paperback
ISBN 978-1-4473-2195-8 ePub
ISBN 978-1-4473-2196-5 Kindle

British Library Cataloguing in Publication Data
A catalogue record for this book is available from the British Library.

Library of Congress Cataloging-in-Publication Data
A catalog record for this book has been requested.

Cover design by Policy Press
Printed in Great Britain by www.4edge.co.uk

ALSO AVAILABLE IN THIS SERIES

GENDER AND FAMILY edited by Viviene E. Cree

THE STATE edited by Viviene E. Cree

MORAL REGULATION edited by Mark Smith

The complete volume, *Revisiting Moral Panics*, including
a commentary by Charles Critcher

Contents

Contributors

Ian Butler is Dean of the Faculty of Humanities and Social Sciences at the University of Bath; he has written extensively on child welfare policy and social work practice. He is a Fellow of the Academy of Social Sciences and an Honorary Member of the Council of the NSPCC. He is the author along with Mark Drakeford of *Social work on trial: The Colwell Inquiry and the state of welfare* (2011).

Gary Clapton is a Senior Lecturer in Social Work at the University of Edinburgh. He specialises in adoption and fostering, child welfare and protection and fathers. His work includes *Social work with fathers: Positive practice* (2013) and a number of papers directed to changing current policies and practices in Scotland.

Viviene E. Cree is Professor of Social Work Studies at the University of Edinburgh. She is a qualified youth and community and social worker. She has carried out extensive research into social work history, the profession and children's services and has published widely. A recent book is *Becoming a social worker: Global narratives* (2013).

Mark Hardy works as a social worker for a local authority children and families practice team in central Scotland. He has previous experience of residential childcare and youth work and has written about recording policy and practice within residential childcare.

Anneke Meyer is a Senior Lecturer in Sociology at Manchester Metropolitan University. She has researched and written in the areas of child sexual abuse and paedophilia, gender and popular culture, childhood and parenting. Her publications include *The child at risk: Paedophiles, media responses and public opinion* (2007) and *Gender and popular culture* (2011), co-authored with Katie Milestone.

Ethel Quayle is a Senior Lecturer in Clinical Psychology at the University of Edinburgh. She has conducted research for many years in technology-mediated crimes, collaborating internationally with government and non-government agencies in the context of research, policy and practice. A recent book, *Internet child pornography: Understanding and preventing on-line child abuse* (2012), is edited with Kurt Ribisl.

Mark Smith is a Senior Lecturer and current Head of Social Work at the University of Edinburgh. He has an interest in abuse allegations made against care staff and is currently working on an ESRC-funded project centred on allegations against the former BBC disc jockey, Jimmy Savile. One of his recent books is *Residential child care in practice: Making a difference* (2013), written with Leon Fulcher and Peter Doran.

E. Kay M. Tisdall is Professor of Childhood Policy and Co-Director of the Centre for Research on Families and Relationships, at the University of Edinburgh. Her academic and policy interests centre on children's rights and childhood studies. Recent papers include 'The transformation of participation? Exploring the potential of "transformative participation" for theory and practice around children and young people's participation', in *Global Studies of Childhood*, vol 3, no 2, pp 183–93.

Joanne Westwood has recently moved from the University of Central Lancashire to an appointment as a Senior Lecturer in the School of Applied Social Science at the University of Stirling. Her research interests are child welfare and children and young people's participation. Her latest publication is 'Childhood in different cultures', in *An introduction to early childhood studies* (2013), edited by Trisha Maynard and Nigel Thomas.

Series editors' preface

Viviene E. Cree, Gary Clapton and Mark Smith

This book series begins and ends with a question: how useful are ideas of moral panic to the social issues and anxieties that confront us today? Forty years on from the publication of Stan Cohen's seminal study *Folk Devils and Moral Panics*, does this remain a helpful way of thinking about social concerns, or should the concept be consigned to the sociological history books as an amusing, but ultimately flawed, theoretical device? 'Moral panic' is, after all, one of the foremost sociological terms that has crossed over from academic to public discourse; in doing so, it has lost a great deal of its rigour and, arguably, its value. All the contributors to the series are, in their own ways, engaging critically with the relevance of moral panic ideas for their own understandings of some of the most pressing personal, professional and political concerns of the day. They do not all come up with the same conclusions, but they do agree that moral panics – no matter how we think of them – focus on the social issues that worry us most.

The book series takes forward findings from an Economic and Social Research Council (ESRC) sponsored research seminar series that ran between 2012 and 2014 at events across the UK. The seminar series was designed to mark the 40th anniversary of *Folk Devils and Moral Panics*; and to bring together international and UK academics, researchers and practitioners from a range of disciplines to debate and discuss moral panics in the 21st century. The three main organisers had, independently of one another, written about events and happenings that had caused great anxiety within social work and within society as a whole: satanic abuse (Clapton, 1993); sex trafficking (Cree, 2008); abuse in residential childcare (Smith, 2008 and 2010). In each case, we had challenged accepted accounts of the issues and asked questions about the real-life (often negative) consequences of holding particular conceptualisations of these difficult topics. We had not, at that time, used the concept of moral panic as the foremost tool for analysis, but we had all been interested in the ideas of discourse, labelling, deviancy amplification and social control, all of which connect with ideas of moral panic. With the 40th anniversary imminent, we saw this as offering an opportunity to revisit this, asking: what relevance does the idea of moral panic have for an examination of 21st-century social issues and anxieties?

The seminar series produced a number of outcomes: articles, blogs and the collection of papers included in these bytes. However, the collection is broader than the seminar series in two key ways: firstly, some chapters were especially commissioned because it was felt that there was a gap in the collection or because the writer had a particularly interesting approach to the issues; secondly, each of the books in this series ends with an afterword written by a social work practitioner who has been invited to reflect on the contributions from the perspective of practice. This demonstrates not only our commitment to knowledge exchange more generally, but also our belief that moral panic ideas have special relevance for social work.

Moral panics and social work

Although 'moral panic' is a sociological idea that has widespread intellectual interest, it has, as Cohen (1998) acknowledges, special relevance for social work. Social work as an academic discipline and a profession plays a central role in the process of defining social issues and then trying to do something about them – that is our job! So we have to be particularly alert to the part we play within this. We are, in moral panic parlance, 'moral entrepreneurs' and 'claims makers': we tell society (government, policy makers, other practitioners, members of the public) what the social problems are, how they should be understood and how they should be addressed. We do so, in 21st-century terms, through secular, professional and academic discourse, but at heart, what we are expressing is a set of ideas about how we should live and what it is to be human. In other words, we remain a 'moral' and, at times, moralising profession.

The concept of moral panic reminds us that our deeply held attitudes and values have origins and consequences in the real world, both positive and negative. And sometimes they are not the origins or consequences we expect them to be. Hence the lens of moral panic highlights the ways in which social issues that begin with real concerns may lead to the labelling and stigmatising of certain behaviours and individuals; they may precipitate harsh and disproportionate legislation; they may make people more fearful and society a less safe place. Focusing on some social issues may distract attention away from other, underlying concerns; so a focus on trafficking may, for example, ignore the realities of repressive, racist immigration policies, just as a focus on internet pornography may lead to legislation that undermines individual freedom, and a focus on child protection may inhibit our capacity to support families, as Featherstone et al (2014) have identified. These are not issues about which we, as editors and contributors to this series, have answers – but we do have questions. And it is our firm belief that social work must engage with these questions if we are to practise in ways that are truly emancipatory and in line with the social work profession's social justice principles.

A particular moment in the history of moral panics?

The years 2013 and 2014 have proved to be a very particular time in the history of moral panics for two, very different, reasons. The first reason is that a number of key protagonists from the early theoretical writing on deviance, moral panics and the state died in 2013 and early 2014.

- Stan Cohen, sociologist and author of *Folk Devils and Moral Panics* (1972), *Visions of Social Control* (1985), *States of Denial* (2001) and numerous other publications, died in January 2013.
- Geoffrey Pearson, social work professor and author of *The Deviant Imagination* (1975) and *Hooligan: A History of Respectable Fears* (1983), died in April 2013.

- Jock Young, criminologist and author of *The Drugtakers* (1971) and many other studies including, most recently, *The Criminological Imagination* (2011), died in November 2013.
- Stuart Hall, critical theorist, founding editor of *New Left Review* and author with Charles Critcher and others of *Policing the Crisis* (1978), died in February 2014.

We wished to mark the contribution of these great thinkers, and so we have included a commentary on one of them within each byte in the series. This is not to suggest that they are the only people who have written about contemporary social issues in this way; in fact, Geoffrey Pearson was more concerned with the persistent nature of what he called 'respectable discontents' than about the sporadic eruptions of moral panics. But, as the series will demonstrate, theorists from a wide range of academic disciplines have continued to engage with the concept of moral panics over the 40-plus years since 1972, sometimes arguing for its continuing value (for example, Goode and Ben-Yehuda, 1994) and at other times favouring alternative explanations, such as those around risk (for example, Beck, 1992, 1999) and moral regulation (for example, Hunt, 1999). More recently, scholars have attempted to move 'beyond the heuristic', to develop a way of thinking about moral panic that both informs, and continues 'to be informed by, movements and developments in social theory' (Rohloff and Wright, 2010, p 419).

The second reason why this has been a special time is because of what has been called the 'Jimmy Savile effect' in numerous press and media reports. It is difficult to discuss the scandal around Jimmy Savile, TV presenter and prolific sex offender, who died in October 2011, in a dispassionate way. In September and October 2012, almost a year after his death, claims emerged that Savile had committed sexual abuse over many years, with his victims ranging from girls and boys to adults. By October 2012, allegations had been made to 13 British police forces, and a series of inquiries followed. The revelations around the Jimmy Savile affair encouraged others to come forward and claim that they had been abused by celebrities: Stuart Hall (TV presenter, not critical theorist), Rolf Harris, Max Clifford and many others have been investigated and prosecuted. These events have encouraged us to ask wider questions in articles and blogs about physical and sexual abuse, and about potentially negative fall-out from the furore around historic abuse. This has not been easy: how do we get across the reality that we are not minimising the damage that abuse can cause, while at the same time calling for a more questioning approach to victimisation and social control? These questions remain challenging as we move forward.

The series

This series of bytes introduces a collection of papers that engage with a social issue through the lens of moral panic. It will be evident from the chapters that, as editors, we have not imposed a 'moral panic straightjacket' on the contributors; nor do we hold to the notion that there is one 'Moral Panic Theory' with a capital T. Instead, contributors have been invited to consider moral panic ideas very broadly, focusing on their capacity to add to a deeper understanding of the social problem under discussion. Because of this, the series offers a number of opportunities for those who are already familiar with the concept of moral panic and for those who are not. For those who have been thinking about moral panic ideas for years, the series will serve as a new 'take' on some of the puzzling aspects of moral panic theories. For those who are coming across the notion of moral panic for the first time, or have only everyday knowledge of it, the case-study examples of particular social issues and anxieties contained in each chapter will serve as an introduction not only to moral panic as a theoretical concept, but also to what, we hope, might become a new avenue of critical inquiry for readers in the future.

The series is divided into four short volumes ('bytes'): *Gender and family*; *Childhood and youth*; *The state*; and *Moral regulation*. Each byte contains an introduction, which includes a short retrospective on one of the four early theorists whom we have already identified. Five chapters follow, each exploring the case study of one social issue, asking how useful a moral panic lens is (or is not) to understanding this social problem. Each byte ends with an afterword written by a social work practitioner. The four bytes are also available as a single volume – *Revisiting moral panics*, featuring an introduction to Moral Panic Theory by Charles Critcher – with the aim of reaching as wide an audience as possible.

The books in this series should be read as an opening conversation. We are not seeking either consensus or closure in publishing this series; quite the opposite, our aim is to ask questions – of social problems, of professional practice and of ourselves. In doing so, we pay homage to Cohen's (1998, p 112) challenge to 'stay unfinished'; instead of seeking to resolve the contradictions and complexities that plague theory and practice, we must, he argues, be able to live with ambiguity. The series may help us and others to do just that, and, in doing so, may contribute towards the building of a more tolerant, open social work practice and a more tolerant, open society.

Acknowledgement

With thanks to the ESRC for funding the seminar series 'Revisiting Moral Panics: A Critical Examination of 21st Century Social Issues and Anxieties' (ES/J021725/1) between October 2012 and October 2014.

References

Beck, U. (1992) *Risk society: Towards a new modernity*, London: Sage.

Beck, U. (1999) *World risk society*, Cambridge: Polity Press.

Clapton, G. (1993) *Satanic abuse controversy: Social workers and the social work press*, London: University of North London Press.

Cohen, S. (1972) *Folk devils and moral panics: The creation of the mods and rockers*, London: MacGibbon and Kee Ltd.

Cohen, S. (1985) *Visions of social control: Crime, punishment and classification*, Cambridge: Polity Press.

Cohen, S. (1998) *Against criminology,* London: Transaction Publishers.

Cohen, S. (2001) *States of denial knowing about atrocities and suffering*, Cambridge: Polity Press.

Cree, V.E. (2008) 'Confronting sex-trafficking: lessons from history', *International Social Work*, vol 51, no 6, pp 763–76.

Featherstone, B., White, S. and Morris, K. (2014) *Re-imagining child protection: Towards humane social work with families*, Bristol: Policy Press.

Goode, E. and Ben-Yehuda, N. (1994) *Moral panics: The Social construction of deviance*, Oxford: Blackwell.

Hall, S., Critcher, C., Jefferson, T., Clarke, J. and Roberts, B. (1978) *Policing the crisis: Mugging, the state and law and order*, London: Macmillan.

Hunt, A. (1999) *Governing morals: A social history of moral regulation*, Cambridge University Press, New York.

Pearson, G. (1975) *The deviant imagination: Psychiatry, social work and social change*, London: Macmillan.

Pearson, G. (1983) *Hooligan: A history of respectable fears,* London: Macmillan.

Rohloff, A. and Wright, S. (2010) 'Moral panic and social theory: beyond the heuristic', *Current Sociology*, vol 58, no 3, pp 403–19.

Smith, M. (2008) 'Historical abuse in residential child care: an alternative view', *Practice: Social Work in Action*, vol 20, no 1, pp 29–41.

Smith, M. (2010) 'Victim Narratives of historical abuse in residential child care: do we really know what we think we know?', *Qualitative Social Work*, vol 9, no 3, pp 303–20.

Young, J. (1971) *The drugtakers: The social meaning of drug use*, London: Paladin.

Young, J. (2011) *The criminological imagination*, Cambridge: Polity Press.

Introduction

Gary Clapton

In common with the other bytes in this series, a key theorist within the 'moral panic' genre is introduced here. Although Geoffrey Pearson does not actually use the term 'moral panic' to outline the social reaction to issues and anxieties, his work has played a key part in the development of thinking around the issue of deviance, especially deviance associated with young people, a central theme within moral panic writings. For this reason, we have chosen to include him in this volume.

Geoffrey Pearson

Geoffrey (Geoff) Pearson was born on 26 March 1943 in Manchester, England and studied moral sciences (Philosophy and Psychology) at Cambridge University. He worked with people with disabilities in Sheffield before going to the London School of Economics to undertake training in psychiatric social work (interestingly, Stan Cohen was also a qualified psychiatric social worker). After qualifying, he returned to Sheffield to practise as a psychiatric social worker. Pearson went on to become a Lecturer in Social Work at Sheffield Polytechnic, and then took up a similar position at University College, Cardiff. It was here that he published his first major work, *The Deviant Imagination* (1975), which examined the ideological underpinnings of a wide range of theories of deviance. This book also established Pearson's critical perspective on many of the policies and attitudes towards young people that were popular at that time, especially those that were built on ideas of young people's dangerousness.

In 1976, Pearson moved to the University of Bradford. Here he wrote *Hooligan: A History of Respectable Fears* (1983), his most influential work; *Hooligan* was voted one of seven 'iconic' studies in British criminology in 2007. In *Hooligan*, Pearson traces the recurrence of explosions of concern about youth crime (we might call them 'moral panics', although he does not). He draws attention to the reality that these explosions of concern are always accompanied by a harping-back to a halcyon time in the past when (supposedly) life was better all round. He argues that there was never a 'golden age'; instead, there will always be 'respectable fears', whether they are centred on the behaviour of hooligans, garrotters, artful dodgers or whoever else is the current focus of fears. (Again, moral panic discourse would call these groups 'folk devils'.)

In 1985, Pearson became Professor of Social Work at Middlesex Polytechnic, and a member of the Central Council for Education and Training in Social Work. He worked on various projects at this time; one was a study of multi-agency policing, commissioned after the Scarman Report of 1981 (this report, into the Brixton riots in London, had emphasised that there were very poor relations between the police and the black community). Pearson went on to publish a study of drug users, entitled *The New Heroin Users* (1987), in which he highlighted that heroin users were often living in areas that were multiply disadvantaged – by poverty, unemployment and poor housing. Pearson moved to Goldsmiths University in 1989 as Professor of Social Work, and later as Professor of Criminology. He was editor of the *British Journal of Criminology* for eight years and a member of the Runciman Inquiry into drugs and the law, which was commissioned by the Police Foundation in 2000 to look at the workings of the UK's Misuse of Drugs Act 1971. He was also vice-chair of the Institute for the Study of Drug Dependency at this time, and continued to conduct empirical research into young people's drug use. Pearson retired in 2008, but went on to chair the Independent Commission on Social Services in Wales; this produced a very critical report in 2010.

This series, concerned as it is with the current social issues and anxieties (the 'respectable fears') of the day, owes allegiance to Pearson's critical thinking and scepticism, as well as, we hope, to his passion. When Pearson was asked to comment on *Hooligan* in 2007, he said: 'I still think *Hooligan* is a stunningly funny book, and I wouldn't change a word of it, other than a few digs at ASBOS, chavs, parenting orders and neighbours from hell' (Berry, 2008: 832).

Geoff Pearson died on 5 April 2013.

Content of this byte

The chapters in Part Two introduce some of the many issues and concerns surrounding young people, children and childhood; what links them is their use of a moral panic perspective (some more explicitly than others) to understand what is going on both in and behind the various anxieties that are discussed. This byte, along with the others in this series, contains chapters that draw from the disciplines of sociology, social policy, psychology and social work. All the chapters highlight the importance of not taking things for granted and of questioning the basis of our beliefs. The social issues identified here all have consequences, often negative ones, for individuals and for society; such is the power of panics.

Chapter One, by Ian Butler, sets out the big picture facing social work and social workers. He outlines the propensity for panic that surrounds social work with children and families, especially when, as is inevitably the case, a tragedy occurs. Professor Butler makes the telling point that, while tragedies frequently happen, it takes a certain conjunction of political and economic conditions for one to become a 'cause célèbre' in which social workers are pilloried as the whipping boys (and girls) for societal consciences, as mediated through the opinion writers and editors of the press.

The remaining four chapters explore how moral panic work might help us to grasp the essence of concerns relating to child trafficking, childhood, the internet and child sexual abuse and, one of the most recent manifestations of alarm, child sexual exploitation. Joanne Westwood's Chapter Two looks at the contemporary concerns surrounding child trafficking. She draws on historical examples of panic surrounding child trafficking and identifies continuities in the ways that the issue was discussed in the 19th century and today, pointing out the sensationalist tones that work to mask the structural causes that underpin trafficking. In Chapter Three Kay Tisdall takes a key aspect of moral panic work, claims making, and subjects a letter to the press to a thorough analysis of the various claims contained within it, the implicit moralising about childhood and good and bad parenting, and considers the various personal claims inherent in the list of signatories. In Chapter Four, about child pornography, Ethel Quayle asks us to look at where our gaze is drawn to and, just as important, where it is drawn away from. Also pointed out is the disproportionate emphasis on the dangers of the internet, to the detriment of its benefits. Chapter Five, by Anneke Meyer, analyses the various contentions, claims and concerns that have arisen in the aftermath of the publication of an inquiry into child sexual exploitation in one UK city.

All of the bytes in this series have subject matter in common, in that material and discussion points about young people, children and childhood will also be found elsewhere, for instance *Gender and the family* has a contribution about moral panics in Italy that include children. In *The state*, the issue of children and the internet is addressed. This is probably inevitable, in that panics about young people and children draw in adults, families and the state. In addition, such panics raise big questions about morals, moralising and those that moralise – the subject matter of *Moral regulation*. Such unifying demonstrates the utility of a moral panic lens. While we do not expect total agreement, we hope that this byte will not only help to illuminate the subject matter covered in the other bytes in the series but also stimulate interest in adopting a greater scepticism when, as is inevitable, a fresh 'urgent' worry about children emerges and makes claims on us.

References

Berry, L. (2008) 'Review of *Hooligan: A History of Respectable Fears*', *British Journal of Social Work*, vol 38, no 4, pp 830–2.

Pearson, G. (1975) *The deviant imagination*, New Jersey: Holmes & Meier Publishers.

Pearson, G. (1983) *Hooligan: A history of respectable fears*, Basingstoke: Macmillan.

Pearson, G. (1987) *The new heroin users*, Oxford: Basil Blackwell.

Scarman, Lord (1981) *The Brixton disorders, 10–12 April 1981*, London: HMSO.

ONE

Child protection and moral panic

Ian Butler

Introduction

> A condition, episode, person or group of persons emerges to become defined as a threat to societal values and interests; its nature is presented in a stylised and stereotypical fashion by the mass media; the moral barricades are manned by editors, bishops, politicians and other right-thinking people; socially accredited experts pronounce their diagnoses and solutions; ways of coping are evolved or (more often) resorted to. (Cohen, 1972, p 9)

As well as providing an enduring and invaluable analytical tool for understanding the politics of control and the manufacture of social order, in this definition of a moral panic Cohen also inadvertently captured almost exactly how working in child protection has felt for the last 30 years. The majority of the children's workforce would recognise the sense of threat; the over-simplifications; the moral outrage; the endless and seemingly futile attempts to 'never let this happen again' and the many, many ways in which countless experts have pointed out how the job might be better done.

This chapter will argue that by applying Cohen's analysis to the social practice of child protection, particularly to those cases that achieve the status of a national 'scandal', we can learn far more about the politics of welfare and the state's relationship to troubled and troublesome families than we can ever learn about how to look after vulnerable children. In particular, it will explore how iconic child deaths can be used to construct a 'condition, episode, person or group of persons

... defined as a threat to societal values and interests' – the idea at the core of what is implied by Cohen's formulation of a moral panic.

Learning from our mistakes

This is not to wholly set aside the improvements in child-protection practice that have derived from the innumerable public inquiry reports, Serious Case Reviews and Individual Management Reviews that have been published over the last 30 years. I would suggest, however, that the gains are increasingly marginal, except in so far as they promote compliance with existing protocols, as most such reports have become formulaic and repetitive.

One might even argue, particularly in relation to the more widely known cases, that they have had the opposite effect as far as protecting children is concerned. For example, the cumulative effect of reporting child abuse by reference only to its most notorious failures, often involving the death of a child, is to reinforce the view that child abuse is sporadic, dramatic and perpetrated only by monsters. We know, on the other hand, that much child abuse is systemic, incredibly ordinary in many ways and perpetrated across the whole social and psychological spectrum.

The consequence of this is that, for at least 30 years, public, political and professional focus has remained on the mechanisms of regulation rather than on the mechanisms of causation as far as child abuse is concerned. Public policy focuses much more on the training and management of the workforce than it does on the causes and correlates of child abuse; practitioners talk about 'safeguarding' but less about 'promoting welfare' (see section 17 of the Children Act 1989) and the popular imagination focuses on the failures of social workers much more frequently than on the failures of the political and social contexts in which they operate.

Where the study of such cases is more useful, perhaps, is in what they tell us about the contemporary state of social work as a form of social practice and about how certain individuals and families are understood and managed by the state. It is in this sense that they can be understood, as per Cohen's original definition, if not as a form, then as instruments of moral panic and, in that sense, part of the politics of control.

Scandals

I have described elsewhere (Butler and Drakeford, 2003; 2005) how scandals are not haphazard events that arise from specific, exceptional practice failures. Rather, they are very likely – if not inevitable – only in very particular circumstances, and they arise, build and subside in a consistent and predictable way.

They arise and fall at key points of transition in societal values and interests and at specific moments in the transition of public policy affecting certain groups of individuals and families; in short, at points of major upheaval in the nature, scope and operation of the welfare state. By the same token, where there is no fundamental tension in a particular policy field or in the societal attitudes and values in which it is embedded, there are no scandals – no matter how grievously young people may suffer. Where scandals do not occur is just as interesting as where they do. For example, broadly speaking, the youth justice 'arms race' since the mid-1990s, whereby successive governments have sought to be tougher on crime and criminals than their predecessors, has met with little opposition, and despite over 20 years of Chief Inspector of Prisons Reports that testify to the endemic bullying, atrocious living conditions and ill-treatment of children and young adults in custody there has been hardly a trace of scandal (Drakeford and Butler, 2007).

It is important therefore to distinguish between the underlying events that form the basis of a scandal and the scandal itself. Scandals do not happen because children die or are seriously harmed at the hands of their parents or those responsible for their care. These may be necessary conditions, but they are far from sufficient.

Children die at the hands of those who are supposed to be looking after them almost every week of the year, every year. These deaths are certainly tragedies, but they are not scandals. Almost all such child deaths remain known to only a small number of relatives and professionals. In that sense, by far the majority of child deaths remain within the relatively private domain. Scandals occur when such routine, almost domestic affairs, become public property in a way that excites sustained or intense interest and that calls for explanation.

Scandals are formed from highly selected cases. It is true that events that become scandalised will often share certain common characteristics; 'pantomime' heroes and villains; a degree of foreignness or the exotic; an element of the macabre; a contradiction between the scene of the scandal and the ostensible purpose of such places (for example, a child is not supposed to be injured by its parents, harmed by its doctor and so on), but even these are not necessary.

In any case, this is not a complete definition of a scandal. So far the events would amount to no more than 'news' and not every child death even makes it into the news. For what might amount to a no more than a news story to become a scandal, the underlying events somehow have to come to be regarded as symptomatic or emblematic of something far more widespread than the specific instance.

What is odd, though, is that what is newsworthy to a wider audience and potential material for a scandal might not appear in the least bit wrong or unusual to those on the 'inside'. In almost all of the welfare scandals since 1965, the events described are to many of those closest to them no more than simply business as usual. What happens is that the events that lie at the core of a scandal take on a significance and a set of meanings that were not obvious to those most closely associated with them. Many of these meanings derive from the underlying, subterranean policy pressures and the transformations that are underway; although they may also become the site across which a whole variety of political and moral hobby-horses are ridden. A number of these have been described in detail elsewhere – the death penalty in Colwell or latent racism in Climbié, for example (Butler and Drakeford, 2003; 2005; 2011).

In that sense, scandals don't just happen, and certainly they don't just happen because things 'go wrong' – things go wrong every day. Scandals are constructed. New meanings are applied to events that are quite different to those applied to the same events by those who inhabit the world in which the scandal originates – it is at this point that the connection between iconic child deaths and Cohen's fundamental account of a moral panic becomes more obvious.

Even when the underlying events are quite clearly outrages in any terms (such as murder or sexual abuse), in order to be scandalised, the events have to be transformed from the familiar and mundane into the public and symbolic, and for that, sustained interest from wider constituencies of interest is critical. That process of transformation begins with discovery. Someone becomes aware of certain events and wants something done about them. They might be a whistle-blower from within an institution, the relative of someone affected by the events at the core of the scandal or a complete outsider with an agenda of their own.

Discovery is not enough, however. The audience for the discovery needs to be widened. The public have to hear and have their interest engaged, and here the media have an important part to play in the construction of a scandal. This presupposes that there is an audience for the scandal. This goes to the heart of the scandalising process, especially when one considers that the events that lie at the heart of a scandal might have gone on for years.

'Why does this matter now?' is the most important question to answer in understanding any scandal. It is at this point that we begin to get a sense of what the fundamental issues are, of which the scandal is merely the outward representation.

One of the key players in the scandal process is the Public Inquiry. Inquiries should not be seen as neutral events. Almost all of them are set up apparently to 'establish the facts', but in doing so the Inquiry is itself an active player in the struggle to make sense of what has happened, adding its own voice to the construction of events. The reports that they produce, the most enduring record of the 'truth' of what happened, in their choice of language, tone and internal structure can add or change our understanding of what the 'facts' were.

Elsewhere and at greater length than this chapter will permit, Mark Drakeford and I have provided many examples of why certain scandals appear and disappear and try to locate them in their sociopolitical context (Butler and Drakeford, 2003; 2005). One of the threads that we have tried to follow in our work is what successive scandals tell us about the state of social work at a particular time. In the Colwell case (Butler and Drakeford, 2011), for example, it was precisely the arriviste and potentially dangerous profession of social work that was 'on trial'. More broadly, however, beyond the tragic circumstances of one child in a particular family, in the hands of Sir Keith Joseph and, later, David Owen, Barbara Castle, James Callaghan and Harold Wilson, the case became an opportunity by which a new set of relationships between the state and its more troubled and troubling families was debated and a site where the architecture of the welfare state was reconfigured in the face of the economic necessities of the 1970s, rather than the 1948 consensus on which it had been built.

While other tensions were debated, such as the death penalty or where the balance should fall in relation to 'tug-of-love' cases, the Colwell scandal was essentially about the difference between a 'problem family' and a 'family with problems' and how the state, and its social workers in particular, should respond in the post-Seebohm, oil-crisis, three-day-week world in which the Colwell case was constructed. It may be worth recalling that it was the Colwell case that paved the way for the first wave of virulent antisocial work media coverage that ran through the reporting of the inquiries into the deaths of Heidi Koseda, Kimberley Carlile and Tyra Henry that clustered after the Jasmine Beckford case and that continued, with occasional lulls, right through the 1980s to the Cleveland Inquiry – a period that saw what one commentator called the emergence of the 'peculiarly British sport of social worker baiting' (Greenland, 1986, p 164).

In terms of Cohen's initial formulation, in this wave of moral panic it was the practice and practitioners of social work as well as certain types of 'problem' family that were clearly identified as the 'condition, episode, person or group of persons' that had emerged 'to become defined as a threat to societal values and interests'.

Peter Connelly and the politics of neoliberalism

The most recent iconic case, that of Peter Connelly, speaks to another set of sociopolitical stresses: the identification of new 'threats' and a new set of moral barricades to erect. In this instance, the process of discovery and the generation of the scandal apparently owed more to the press than to an inquiry, a court judgment or a specific 'outsider' (but see Jones, 2014 for a compelling and disturbing account of the web of political and journalistic intrigue that surrounds this case). Space does not permit a detailed exploration of how the worst excesses of tabloid reporting woefully and reprehensibly wove a web of meaning around a child's tragic death, largely for immediate political purposes of their own. There was the familiar virulent misogyny aimed at the key protagonists; the implicit racism in the tabloid accounts that lingered over what was portrayed as the sinister and foreign-sounding consultant who had failed to diagnose Peter Connelly's severe spinal injuries; and there was much of the 'political correctness gone mad' theme that was perhaps best summed up in the *Sun*'s 14 November 2008 headline 'Incompetent, politically correct and anti-white'.

More importantly for our purposes, the Connelly case provided an important illustration of and an opportunity to justify a marked shift in societal attitudes towards the kinds of families that Peter Connelly's came to typify and to signal a decisive shift in the politics of welfare.

Even at the point where the Connelly case entered the media (through a heated exchange between the Prime Minister, Gordon Brown and David Cameron, the Leader of the Opposition, on 12 November 2008 as part of Prime Minister's Questions in the UK Parliament), the symbolic nature of the case took precedence over the mere facts and even over the child himself:

> Let's be clear. This is a story [sic] about a 17 year old girl who had no idea how to bring up a child. It is about a boyfriend who could not read but could beat a child, and it's about a social services department that gets £100M per year and cannot look after children. (*Hansard*, 2008)

The potential of the Connelly case to provide the embodiment of the 'Broken Britain' narrative that Cameron hints at here and that was to become important in the Conservative Party's 2010 general election campaign was eloquently captured in an article in the *Observer* in August 2009 (Anthony, 2009). Here, the 'bland and unremarkable … shabby pre-war slice of suburbia' that was Connelly's home is revealed to contain

> all the potent symbols and sordid realities of the feckless, desensitised version of contemporary life.
>
> Hardcore pornography, internet chat sites, vodka bottles, attack dogs, animal faeces, fleas, lice, Nazi paraphernalia, knives and replica guns formed the harsh backdrop to Peter's truncated life and brutal death.

The two families at the heart of Anthony's narrative:

> were always unlikely to heal each other's brutalised psyches and self-inflicted wounds. When they came together, they instead turned a grim domestic drama into a social tragedy that reverberated far beyond the squalid confines of their semi-detached Tottenham home.

Part of Anthony's message is the same as Cameron's: that this is not so much a failure by the welfare state, in the person of the hapless social worker, but a failure of the welfare state in that it was the welfare state that created families such as that in which Peter Connelly lived and died:

> it is also a function of a welfare system that allocates subsidies and material security to those with children. The noble intention is to arrest economic deprivation at birth, yet too often it helps foster the very conditions it seeks to combat. The more the state intervenes, the

more it is required to intervene and therefore the more chance that its intervention will, as in the case of Baby P, not be enough.... There is no easy solution to the societal malaise this case highlights, but the fact remains, as many social workers will testify, there is a growing class of state dependants who have gained few if any life skills other than an ability to work the system.

To a limited degree, social work is again a focus for opprobrium but, in reality, it is not a major casualty – at least as a profession. While social workers were busying themselves over which College not to join and sorting out their HCPC from their SWRB application forms, the profession had already moved to the political margins. The real focus of the Connelly scandal, those around whom a panic was being engendered, to return to the specific theme of this chapter, are the individuals and families that social work once sought to help, to empower and on whose behalf the profession once advocated.

After the general election of May 2010, the rhetoric, used both in the media and politically to invoke such families became much more shrill and unpleasant and perhaps reached its peak around the introduction, in December 2011, of the 'Troubled Families' project (TFP) (see Butler, 2014 for a more detailed account). The TFP was seen by Prime Minister Cameron as part of the 'social recovery' that he believed Britain needed as much as any economic 'recovery'. According to Cameron, 'while the government's immediate duty is to deal with the budget deficit my mission in politics – the thing I am really passionate about – is fixing the responsibility deficit' (Cabinet Office, 2011).

The TFP was to be as much an exercise in remoralising as it was in welfare selectivity. Beyond that, it is also an exercise in reframing the general perception of those at the margins of society as somehow responsible for their own conditions and beyond the capacity or the willingness of the state to help, precisely as Anthony's article in the *Observer* had suggested and which the Connelly case seemed to exemplify.

It is not necessary to elaborate here the glee with which the right-wing press in the UK echoed and amplified these sentiments as it awaited the arrival of the 'crack teams' that would soon 'turn up at people's homes to get them out of bed for work, make sure their children go to school or ensure alcoholics or drug addicts go to rehab' (*Daily Mail*, 18 October 2011; see also Jensen, 2013).

Of course the proximate origins of the TFP lay in the riots of the summer of 2011. However, it is important to note the continuity in tone and language in the media representation of the TFP at its launch and subsequently. It is an extension of what Tyler (2013, para 3.1) tellingly calls the 'scum semiotics' that characterised political and media accounts of the 2011 riots.

The subterranean currents that flowed in and out of the 2011 riots and into the TFP run deep in the politics of neoliberalism and signal a decisive move away from Keynesian economics, post-war collectivism and welfare universalism that has characterised much of the politics of the global North in the last 20 years. Indeed, curbing the 'social turmoil generated at the foot of the urban order by public policies of market deregulation and social welfare retrenchment' (Wacquant, 2010, p 210) is a significant structural innovation and a 'major transnational political project' (Wacquant, 2010, p 213) (see also Bauman, 2004; Harvey, 2005; Davies, 2011).

This is a great deal for one short life and brutal death to carry.

Conclusion

Scandals such as the Connelly case provide a biography; a photograph; an address; a real life story around which opinions and attitudes can crystallise to fuel or signal the development of a moral panic. Their lasting value is not in developing the capacity to protect children but to alert us to the interests, motives and agendas of those who express moral outrage and to the varied analyses of 'politicians and other right-thinking people' who will in turn 'pronounce their diagnoses and solutions'.

This is why there will always be welfare scandals; not because professional practice is infinitely perfectible but because the state continuously defines and redefines its relationship to certain of its citizens, particularly those who, arguably, need its protection most.

References

Anthony, A. (2009) 'The killers of Baby P came from decades of abuse and dysfunction', *Observer* (16 August).

Bauman, Z. (2004) *Wasted lives: Modernity and its outcasts*, Cambridge: Polity Press.

Butler, I. (2014) 'New families, new governance and old habits', *Journal of Social Welfare and Family Law*, vol 36, no 4, pp 415–25.

Butler, I. and Drakeford, M. (2003) *Social policy, social welfare and scandal: How British public policy is made*, London: Palgrave Macmillan.

Butler, I. and Drakeford, M. (2005) *Scandal, social policy and social welfare* (2nd rev. edn), Bristol: Policy Press/BASW.

Butler, I. and Drakeford, M. (2011) *Social work on trial: The Colwell Inquiry and the state of welfare*, Bristol: Policy Press.

Cabinet Office (2011) *Troubled Families Speech*, www.gov.uk/government/speeches/troubled-families-speech

Cohen, S. (1972) *Folk devils and moral panics*, London: MacGibbon and Kee.

Daily Mail (2011) 'Helping 100,000 troubled families has saved the taxpayer £1.2BILLION by cutting crime and benefits, says Eric Pickles', *Daily Mail* (18 October), www.dailymail.co.uk/news/article-2988128/Helping-100-000-troubled-families-saved-taxpayer-1-2BILLION-cutting-crime-benefits-says-Eric-Pickles

Davies, J.S. (2011) *Challenging governance theory: From networks to hegemony*, Bristol: Policy Press.

Drakeford, M. and Butler, I. (2007) 'Everyday tragedies: justice, scandal and young people in contemporary Britain', *Howard Journal of Criminal Justice*, vol 46, no 3, pp 219–325.

Greenland, C. (1986) 'Inquiries into child abuse and neglect (CAN) deaths in the United Kingdom', *British Journal of Criminology*, vol 26, no 2, pp 164–72.

Hansard (2008) House of Commons Debate (28 November), *Hansard*, vol 482, part 162, col 762.

Harvey, D. (2005) *A brief history of neoliberalism*, Oxford: Oxford University Press.

Jensen, T. (2013) 'Riots, restraint and the new cultural politics of wanting', *Sociological Research Online*, vol 18, no 4, www.socresonline.org.uk/18/4/7.html

Jones, R. (2014) *The story of Baby P: Setting the record straight*, Bristol: Policy Press.

Tyler, I. (2013) 'The riots of the underclass? Stigmatisation, mediation and the government of poverty and disadvantage in neoliberal Britain', *Sociological Research Online*, vol 18, no 4, p 6, www.socresonline.org.uk/18/4/6.html

Wacquant, L. (2010) 'Crafting the neoliberal state: Workfare, prisonfare and social insecurity' *Sociological Forum* vol 25, no 2, pp 197–220.

TWO

Unearthing melodrama: moral panic theory and the enduring characterisation of child trafficking

Joanne Westwood

Introduction

The issue of child trafficking came to prominence in the early part of the 21st century as international migrations of children became more visible in the UK, attracting the attention of non-governmental organisations (NGOs), politicians and the national news media. The trafficking of children is not a new phenomenon; in the late 19th century campaigners were successful in lobbying for an increase in the age of consent, partially as a result of the media exposé of the 'white slave trade' orchestrated by the newspaper editor William Stead (Bristow, 1978). The phenomenon of child trafficking has also been previously characterised as a moral panic (Goode and Ben-Yehuda, 1994; Cree et al, 2012). Moral panic writings go some way towards explaining the conditions that provide fertile ground for the amplification of risk that is embedded in media representations and policy discourses associated with child trafficking. This chapter will illustrate how the issue of child trafficking continues to be defined, drawing on a model developed from the literary genre of melodrama. The chapter discusses the features of a moral-panic perspective that are relevant to understanding the construction of child trafficking.

What makes this a moral panic?

Moral-panics thinking was originally used to explain the crisis in policing of young people (Cohen, 1972) and has been applied to many social issues in the intervening period (Goode and Ben-Yehuda, 1994; Critcher, 2003). Thompson (1998) identifies a number of common features of a moral panic: there is a campaign or a crusade over a period of time; the issues appeal to those who are concerned in some way about social breakdown; there is a lack of clarity in moral guidelines; politicians and the media are found to be at the head of public debates; and, finally, the real causes of the problems that give rise to a moral panic remain unaddressed. Factors of central importance in understanding an issue as a moral panic are that concerns about behaviour are met with increasing hostility and the issue becomes publicly visible. The issue is represented in disproportionate terms, in that the groups who push social concerns up the political and public agenda do so by constructing the issue as good versus evil and heighten sensitivity by focusing on the worst-case scenario as if it were representative (Thompson, 1998).

Goode and Ben-Yehuda (1994) applied a discussion of moral panic theory to a child trafficking event in Orleans in France in May 1969. Moral panic theory has also previously been drawn on to explain the way in which the 'white slave trade' appeared on the 19th- and 20th-century policy agendas (Doezema, 2001). Methods used by the reform campaigners of the late 19th century had a strong influence on feminist politics and campaigning, particularly those used by the reformer Josephine Butler and her supporters, including the infamous editor of *The Pall Mall Gazette*, William Stead, who ran the infamous exposé: The Maiden Tribute of Modern Babylon Series (Gorham, 1978; Walkowitz, 1992). In more recent work Cree et al (2012) examine this event and the establishment of the UK's Child Exploitation and Online Protection Centre (CEOPS) through a moral panic lens and argue that the emphasis then as now is on the sexual-exploitation aspects of trafficking; other more mundane and less sensationalist reasons for trafficking – domestic care and agricultural work, for example, tend to be overshadowed.

Scale of the problem and proportionality of the response

Despite the development of UK policy responses and the publication of *The UK Action Plan on Tackling Human Trafficking* (Home Office and Scottish Executive 2007) and the practice guidance *Working together to safeguard children who may have been trafficked* (HM Government, 2011), the research literature on the issue of child trafficking in the UK is sparse. A feature of UK NGO publications is a reliance on press reports as evidence of the phenomenon of child trafficking. HM Government (2011) reports that around 300 children are trafficked into the UK annually, and issues a warning that numbers will increase as agencies understand the signs of child trafficking:

> there may be little evidence of any pre-existing relationship between the child and the accompanying adult or even no knowledge about the person who will care for the child. There may be unsatisfactory accommodation in the UK, or perhaps no evidence of parental permission for the child to travel to the UK or stay with the sponsor. These irregularities may be the only indication that the child could be a victim of trafficking (HM Government, 2011, pp 7–8).

The issue of children coming to the UK is therefore understood as a problem because children are separated from their parents, families and communities; this distance between and separateness from their origins and immediate family is perceived in policy terms as being laden with risks and vulnerabilities.

The conditions in which it took place

In relation to the causes of child trafficking, the policy approaches are overly reliant on simplistic demand/supply explanations of child trafficking, or familial dysfunction, and are particularly associated with trafficking for commercial sexual exploitation and, as a result, draw heavily on the language of child protection where children are 'groomed' or otherwise constructed as witless victims. This position obscures the need for a more detailed analysis of children's experiences: the ways in which children arrive into the UK, closer examination of the relationships between children and the people who bring them; and the variety of factors that promote children's migrations. UK policy approaches to date towards migrant children coming without or with their families reflect a desire to protect and sustain a rigid asylum and immigration system. These measures are ostensibly designed to stop independent migrations because of the potential risks of trafficking and future exploitation.

These policies were all developed within a wider political context of increased border control and national security, and were enacted in order to address the perceived threat of immigration and international terrorism. Additionally, the economic threats to the UK of unchecked immigration were emphasised. The immigration context of policy making has come in for sharp criticism from anti-trafficking organisations and agencies, and there are widely expressed concerns that these responses do not address the trafficking in children because of the hidden nature of the crime and the exploitation children are said to experience. There have been some notable exceptions in the dominant discourse from individuals and state actors who challenge the view that child trafficking is a massive and hidden social problem, and, while these do bring some measured observations to policy debates, they remain minimised and the emphasis remains on immigration and 'safeguarding' at the expense of providing support to meet needs.

Folk devils

Traffickers are depicted as wicked and evil and the narrative in policy documents suggests that trafficking is a global organised trade run by ruthless criminal gangs. There are baddies (the traffickers) and goodies (the victims and the child rescuers). Conversely, the families in children's countries of origin are also depicted as part of the problem of child trafficking. Witless poor, ignorant parents who sell their children into a life of slavery (at worst) or send them to an unknown future in a foreign country with a distant relative or stranger are common explanations found in policy documents and in media reports about child trafficking. These explanations lack context and simplify what are traditional, complicated and reciprocal international familial relationships, obligations and duties that sustain communities and promote cohesion. Children coming to the UK in such circumstances are not sold and their relationships with their families in their countries of origin remain important. The ideology of the family that is promoted in the anti-trafficking policy narratives and media reports is of a specific form and bears little resemblance to a wider understanding of the constitutions of family forms found in different parts of the world.

Claims makers and moral entrepreneurs

Certain groups gain prestige and status and have 'vested interests' in exposing and exaggerating levels of concern about child trafficking. In the UK the NGOs that are party to national and international governmental anti-trafficking activities could be said to have a vested interest in terms of advancing their agendas, and they have previously advocated protective policy measures based on single and extreme cases (that is, the death of Victoria Climbié in London while in the care of her great aunt, to whom she was entrusted by her Côte d'Ivoire parents). The absence of an informed and academic debate on the subject has left space for the emergence of stories about child trafficking that have little basis in reality. The issuing of policy guidance and Home Office-commissioned training, as well as heightened sensitivity, publicity and awareness campaigns orchestrated by NGOs and the media, combine to raise the profile of child trafficking as a growing moral and child-protection threat that requires immediate and sustained action.

Many of the references to risks found in NGO reports about child trafficking are uncritically reproduced in policy documents and guidance. Statements about the hidden harm and the potentially significant numbers of children thought to be at risk of trafficking are also commonplace in the policy discourses. The true scale of the issue is unknown, but commentators and politicians have argued that it is potentially enormous. For example, in October 2004 during a parliamentary debate on the subject of child trafficking, Mr John Bercow, the MP for Buckingham, suggested that parliamentary attention had been "woefully inadequate to the scale of the challenge that we face" (Bercow, 2004). Bercow illustrates the dangers parents are exposing their children to:

> The high profile case of Victoria Climbié, who was trafficked to the UK by her aunt in order to commit benefit fraud … is the tip of the iceberg.… Parents must be made aware that they are not sending their children to a better life when they put them in the hands of traffickers. (Bercow, 2004)

Consequences of the moral panic about child trafficking

As well as highlighting the more sensationalist aspects of the issue, that is, the exploitation and harm, the construction of risk in this way prioritises certain interventions over others. Potential child-trafficking scenarios gain status and determine interventions that might ordinarily be intrusive and disruptive to families. The means are therefore justified by the ends. In policy and practice, children arriving in the UK attract suspicion and interest from immigration and child-safeguarding officials. It is not viewed as essential to have proof or evidence of child trafficking. The fact that families come into the UK as asylum seekers or refugees and children come into the UK unaccompanied is enough to arouse the interest of officials. In their efforts to stop trafficking, advocates and anti-trafficking campaigners have thus legitimised policy, and practice is focused on all groups of migrant children.

In the UK child-trafficking policy discourses are underpinned with harm-prevention and risk-management narratives. More recently, in welfare policies generally, the victim has become a high priority, while certain highly valued ideologies of childhood persist in wider policy discourses. The values and priorities of the policy discourses in terms of child trafficking are emphasised in the narratives of home and family and loss and betrayal. The crisis narratives evident in child-trafficking policy-making discourses also convey a need for urgent and immediate action: something must be done. In addition, what is known about child trafficking is only the tip of the iceberg.

It is clear in the policy discourses that the migration of children poses individual risks to children and wider risks in terms of the UK's border security, and in terms of their vulnerability to being sexually exploited. Critically, child trafficking has come to be understood as being about wider societal and, particularly, sexual threats to children as well as about 'innocent and helpless victims' (Buckland, 2008). In relation to trafficking in women and children the domination of a 'victim trope' together with the positioning of men as predators, abusers, exploiters or crime bosses, legitimates restrictive and punitive policies, again an approach that underestimates the structural factors that lead to migrations (Buckland, 2008, p 43).

Discussion

Although the activities of the 19th-century social puritans and current anti-trafficking activities might be explained as a moral panic (Cohen, 1972) or as a moral crusade (Goode and Ben-Yehuda 1994), this does not fully account for the way in which the risks have been constructed and reconstructed across the historically different contexts. The amplification of risk is a central and enduring feature in moral-panic writings, and risk is amplified in the case of child trafficking using melodramatic tactics. Melodramatic tactics, according to Hadley (1995), are characterised by portrayals of five key themes: familial narratives of dispersal and reunion; visual rendering of bodily torture and criminal conduct; atmospheric menace and providential plotting; expressions of highly charged emotions; and a tendency to personify absolutes like good and evil. Melodramatic tactics are evident in the 19th-century social-purity campaigning activities, serialised style and pseudo-factual story-telling to convey to an unsuspecting public the tragic situations of victims through emotional appeals and righteous indignation. This was a popularised late 19th-century protest format, peculiar to social purity groups of that period (Walkowitz, 1992), and these tactics are evident in their campaigning publications. The concept of melodramatic tactics has further analytical value as applied to contemporary policy and legislation about the issue of child trafficking.

A common strategy in the melodrama of protest is the attempt to amplify concern through the creation of a 'blameless victim':

> to pinpoint a contemporary evil they set up a blameless hero as the victim of the system, and then subject him to such inhuman persecution that the audience explodes with indignation and demands the immediate repeal of laws which perpetuate such cruelties. (Smith, 1973, p 75)

There is only a limited acknowledgement of the 'harms' and 'risks' associated with intractable problems of war, oppression and poverty that are characteristic features of the countries children originate from. The complexities of child migration seemed to be little understood and do not appear as important or relevant in the policy narratives; what is important is tackling the criminal activities of (criminalised) others. Global structural factors that influence migratory flows are avoided, minimised in the narratives, the emphasis being on tackling the crimes of exploitation, and protecting, indeed rescuing, children from the clutches of wicked criminal gangs. These modern melodramatic tactics are also found in the media exposures of child trafficking that are designed to scandalise and shock audiences. This is hardly surprising, given that the media tend to rely upon anti-trafficking NGOs as 'authoritative' sources of information. These melodramatic tactics are evident in parliamentary papers, which are also informed by NGO evidence and provide campaigners with ammunition to lobby for greater protection and, ultimately, restrictions on the migratory movements of children to the UK. The global social inequalities that push children into migration may be occasionally articulated, although this is often to a much lesser extent in the campaigning materials, and the overwhelming emphasis is on exposing and re-exposing the crime, the villains and a 'suffering children' experience.

Conclusion

There is no doubt that children are brought to the UK and are exploited and abused here. The numbers of children subjected to exploitation in this way are small, and yet policy responses have been swift and all-encompassing in terms of both preventing children from coming into the UK and the depth of official suspicion of those who successfully navigate their way here. The policy responses to child trafficking as discussed in this chapter are disproportionate to the issue and suggest that the problem is widespread and growing, with countless numbers of children at risk or vulnerable to being trafficked.

The UK establishment, media, policy makers and anti-trafficking campaigners in the 21st century have employed well-rehearsed methods for characterising child trafficking as a moral issue, using melodramatic tactics to arouse public indignation and anger at the exploitation of innocent victims, the historical precursors being evident in the 19th-century campaigns against the 'white slave trade'. It is of course also worth remembering that the organisations that lead these campaigns and maintain public awareness of the abuse and exploitation of children more broadly have a vested interest in ensuring that their work remains high profile. Many of these organisations receive huge amounts of funding to train social workers, and develop toolkits to support child victims, and thus their role is not unbiased.

Melodramatic tactics have further analytical value when examining more broadly child welfare and child abuse issues that are becoming a semi-permanent feature of moral panics as stories of the historical abuse of children dominate the news headlines and arouse public anger and politicians' wrath.

References

Bercow, J. (2004) *Hansard*, 21 October, c.1116–c.1117, www.publications.parliament.uk/pa/cm200304/cmhansrd/vo041021/debtext/41021–32.htm#41021–32_spnew8 (accessed 1 June 2014).

Bristow, E. (1978) *Vice and vigilance: Purity movements in Britain since 1700*, Dublin: Gill and Macmillan.

Buckland, B.S. (2008) 'More than just victims: the truth about human trafficking', *Public Policy Research*, vol 15, no 1, pp 42–7.

Cohen, S. (1972) *Folk devils and moral panics*, London: McGibbon and Kee.

Cree, V., Clapton, G. and Smith, M. (2012) 'The presentation of child trafficking in the UK: an old and new moral panic?', *British Journal of Social Work*, vol 44, no 2, pp 418–33.

Critcher, C. (2003) *Critical readings: Moral panics and the media: issues in cultural and media studies*, Buckingham: Open University Press.

Doezema, J. (2001) 'Ouch! Western feminists' "wounded attachment" to the "third world prostitute"', *Feminist Review*, vol 67, pp 16–38.

Goode, E. and Ben-Yehuda, N. (1994) *Moral panics: The social construction of deviance*, London: Blackwell.

Gorham, D. (1978) 'The "maiden tribute of modern Babylon" re-examined: child prostitution and the idea of childhood in late Victorian England', *Victorian Studies*, vol 21, pp 354–79.

HM Government (2011) *Safeguarding children who may have been trafficked*, London: Department for Education and the Home Office, https://www.gov.uk/government/uploads/system/uploads/attachment_data/file/177033/DFE-00084-2011.pdf.

Hadley, E. (1995) *Melodramatic tactics. Theatricalised dissent in the English marketplace, 1800–1885*, California: Stanford University Press.

Home Office and Scottish Executive (2007) *The UK Action Plan on Tackling Human Trafficking*, Norwich: The Stationery Office.

Smith, J.L. (1973) *Melodrama: The critical idiom*, London: Methuen and Co. Ltd.

Thompson, K. (1998) *Moral panics*, Abingdon: Routledge.

Walkowitz, J.R. (1992) *City of dreadful delights. Narratives of sexual danger in late-Victorian London*, London: Virago.

THREE

Lost childhood?

Kay Tisdall

Introduction

The trope of 'lost childhood' is a recurring one within UK newspapers. Every few years, a news article, editorial or letter leads with this idea, causing some media interest and connected articles, but then fades away until the next time. For those in childhood studies, the trope is familiar, drawing on adults' idealisations of childhood based around children's 'pricelessness', innocence and vulnerability. A less familiar way to consider the trope is through the lens of moral panic theory. This chapter brings together concepts from moral panics and childhood studies to help analyse this 'lost childhood' trope. As Garland writes, sociologists using the concepts of moral panics start with scepticism that 'permits the initial observation' to give 'way to a different attitude – one that is more analytic, more explanatory, or perhaps better, more diagnostic' (Garland, 2008, p 21).

The chapter uses one particular example of the 'lost childhood' media articles, a letter published on 23 September 2011 in the UK newspaper the *Telegraph*. The article was titled the 'Erosion of childhood', with the sub-title 'Here is the full letter from more than 200 experts about how childhood is being eroded by a "relentless diet" of advertising and addictive computer games'. The letter was concerned about 'too much, too soon' for children, particularly in relation to 'increasing commercial pressures', starting formal education too early and spending time indoors with screen-based technology. The letter cited the UNICEF (2007) publication on children's well-being (where the UK was ranked at the bottom of 21 OECD countries) as key evidence. It made policy recommendations, including information campaigns on children's developmental needs and avoiding a 'consumerist screen-based life-style', establishing a play-based curriculum in nurseries and primary schools, encouraging outdoor play and connection with nature, and banning marketing directed at children up to the age of seven. Two hundred and twenty-eight people signed the letter.

The following discussion brings together relevant concepts from moral panics – that is, the stages of moral panics and, particularly, 'moral entrepreneurs' – to (re)consider the letter. It will end by reflecting on the implications of the letter's moral claims and the usefulness of moral panic theory to consider this media trope of 'lost childhood'.

Stages to moral panics

Critcher suggests eight stages to moral panics, with respective constituents:

1. Emergence	New and threatening development
2. Media inventory	Stereotyping via folk devils/sensationalism/sensitisation
3. Moral entrepreneurs	Moralisation by pressure groups/politicians/religious leaders/press
4. Experts	Expert confirmation of dangers
5. Elite consensus	Public marginalised/opposition weak
6. Coping and resolution	New laws and/or stricter enforcement
7. Fade away	Volatility with possible reoccurrence
8. Legacy	Moral boundaries and established discourse confirmed (Critcher, 2012).

The 'lost childhood' trope can be traced through the UK media in recent years,[1] including this letter of 2011. It does not, however, move through all of Critcher's eight stages. The first stage, emergence, is evident as the trope positions itself against threatening developments:

in the case of this letter, a number of concerns like the UK's low score on children's well-being, high levels of teenage distress and disaffection and consumer pressure on children are present. The letter draws strongly on stages 3 and 4, with what appears to be moralising by moral entrepreneurs, claims to expertise and use of experts. But media interest tends to fade away in a day or two; there are no evident links to new laws, nor stricter enforcement. The trope, then, could be seen as a potential moral panic that never happened (Jackson, 2013). Or it could be a micro-panic, drawing on the idea discussed by McRobbie and Thornton (1995): difficulties in mobilising societal fears and concerns, in a multi-mediated world with multiple voices, lead to a multiplicity of micro-issues and micro-panics, rather than 'classic', fully fledged moral panics (see Goode, 2012).

Moral entrepreneurs

Clapton and colleagues (2013) write about 'moral entrepreneurs' and 'claims-makers' as similar concepts, arising from Cohen (1972) and Jenkins (1992), respectively. Moral entrepreneurs or claims makers involve themselves in 'moralising projects, campaigns and crusades that contribute to the genesis of a moral panic' (Clapton et al, 2013, p 804). They seek to extend the reach of their expertise, in a net-widening effect (Clapton et al, 2013, p 805). The letter makes it easy to consider the moral entrepreneurs and the claims makers in this particular example. The text, and the accompanying story, did not originate in the *Telegraph*; a core group of people organised the letter, recruited others to sign and then submitted it to the newspaper.

All signatories use a first name and a surname. They then differ on whether they give a formal prefix (usually only if Professor or Doctor), their position (for example Chief Executive or MP), and/or an organisational affiliation. Many people put forward more than one affiliation or disciplinary connection. Of the 228 signatories, over one-third connect themselves to a university position, while a further number state a university affiliation. Seven people affiliate themselves with teachers' unions, while at least 26 affiliate themselves with a voluntary organisation or charitable trust. But the largest number do not have a clear organisational connection, instead describing themselves as consultants or by profession (for example, general practitioner). In terms of profession or disciplinary focus, at least 20% are connected to psychology, developmental psychology or psychotherapy, while 25% are connected to play, early years or education.

Twenty-six people (11%) describe themselves as authors (and a further two are well-known fiction writers). Some authors write literary fiction (for example, Phillip Pullman), while others write advice books or accessible non-fiction about children. A smattering of other signatories include politicians, police and religious figures. Only three people identify themselves as a parent or grandparent. It is not evident that any child signed the letter.

The identities chosen by signatories suggest particular forms of claims making. The predominance of academic and professional positions subtly stresses expertise and professionalism: here are experts in their fields. The signatories largely do not appeal to political identities, with few signatories describing themselves as politicians: this letter is 'above party politics', 'speaking professional truth to power'.[2] The few signatories who *do* identify themselves as a grandparent or parent highlight that *most* do not. Many more of the 228 signatories are likely to be parents or grandparents, but this is an identity that most do not foreground. Considering the above, the letter puts forward the signatories as authoritative and persuasive *as experts*. This is recognised by the *Telegraph*'s strapline, which refers to '200 experts'.

Yet, the letter also seeks to appeal more widely. The evidence cited in the letter is from UNICEF and 'international league tables' but the letter goes on to make claims about parents being 'deeply concerned' about the erosion of childhood in Britain since 2006. It refers to 'our children' being subjected to increasing commercial pressures. In the final paragraph the letter asserts that 'It is everyone's responsibility to challenge policy-making and cultural developments', and a unified voice 'from the grass roots' is required. The letter thus moves from referring generally to evidence, which does have a research base, to claims about parents and 'our children' that are rhetorical (with no evidence base cited), to positioning itself from the grassroots. The letter thus progresses from a stance of expertise to seeking to depict itself as a grassroots movement. This skilful development in three paragraphs provides an appealing and persuasive narrative.

The morality within the trope

Garland reminds us of the *moral* in 'moral panics', two elements that he argues as essential to Cohen's original concept:

> (i) the moral dimension of the social reaction, particularly the introspective soul-searching that accompanies these episodes; and (ii) the idea that the deviant conduct in question is somehow *symptomatic*. (Garland, 2008, p 11)

What moral concerns are evident in the letter? And how are the concerns, the deviant conduct, symptomatic of broader issues?

To those who read the classics in the childhood studies' literature, the letter makes very familiar appeals. For example, Zelizer wrote a seminal book in 1985, titled *Pricing the Priceless Child: The Changing Social Value of Children*. Writing about the US, she suggests that children's contributions to households are economically worthless but emotionally 'priceless'. Children's value lies in their ability to give meaning and fulfilment to their parents' lives. For parents, protecting their children, protecting the 'preciousness of childhood', seeking to provide their own children with the 'perfect childhood' freed from adult worries and concerns, gives them meaning and fulfilment. Jenks (1996) writes of prevailing, dichotomous perceptions of childhood, which he labels Dionysian and Apollonian. The former considers children as inherently sinful, needing constraint; the latter perceives children as innocent, needing nurturance. The innocent child is frequently associated with Rousseau (writing in the 18th century) and ideas about children being inherently closer to nature, and subsequent ideas about childcare and education (see James et al, 1998).

These well-rehearsed constructions of childhood are evident in the letter. The nostalgic ideas of childhood preciousness and innocence are demonstrated by the concerns about children having 'too much, too soon' and 'growing up too quickly'. Instead, to draw on Rousseau-like ideas, children should be outdoors, playing and 'connected to nature'. The letter expresses a particular concern about modern technology, which in the second paragraph becomes narrowed to 'screen-based technology' and is frequently paired with commercial pressures. Children should be protected from such technology and commercialisation, kept away rather than empowered to engage with it (see Buckingham, 2011 for a discussion of childhood constructions within consumer culture).

Childhood studies makes a distinction between children and childhood. Individual children are at a particular life stage and most will grow out of being children, in due course. They may remain relationally someone's children but, at least in the UK, will become legally and socially 'adults'. Childhood, in contrast, is a permanent feature of social structures, one that can be analysed generationally (Qvortrup, 2009). As described above, the letter is more about a particular notion of childhood than about individual children.

Indeed, the letter can be characterised, following Zelizer and Jenks, as being more about parenthood, adulthood and societal concerns than about childhood itself. For example, Hendrick (1997) writes insightfully about childhood in the 19th century, where health, child development and educational interests focused on children as 'the future of the nation' (influenced by the official discovery of the poor health of potential British recruits to the Boer War). Similarly, the letter refers to international league tables (UNICEF's well-being, teenage distress and disaffection), suggesting children's poor showing in international comparisons – and, presumably, international competition. The second paragraph of the letter starts 'Although parents are deeply concerned about this issue ...'; it does not start with children having concerns about this issue, citing no evidence directly from children. In web comments on the letter, contributors write vociferously about the responsibilities and irresponsibility of parents and teachers. In this way, the letter is symptomatic of wider concerns about parenting, societal functioning and 'the future of the nation'.

The letter largely does not appeal to another trope within the UK, that of children's human rights and dignity (see Tisdall, 2014). There is mention in the final paragraph about the need to 'find a more human way to nurture and empower all our children'. Empowerment has connections with social movements and freedom from oppression (see Teamey and Hinton, 2014), but it also has been criticised for being unduly individualistic and failing to confront institutional and structural power sufficiently (Cornwall and Brock, 2005). The particular expression in the letter is 'top-down', suggesting that children will be empowered, rather than empower themselves. The letter does not discuss children's on-going contributions to their families, households and communities, and there is no mention of agency – a key concept within childhood studies that recognises children as social actors (see James, 2009; Oswell, 2013). These moral claims, therefore, are not made.

The letter instead appeals to particular constructions of childhood. These constructions of an *idealised* childhood, a version of which may have existed for some children in some places (and indeed for some of the adults signing the letter). But historical and global evidence of children and childhood shows that childhood was and is often a time of work as well as of play, of experiencing the hardships of poverty, illness and disability, conflict and violence as well as of learning and affection (Cunningham, 2005; Wells, 2009). The letter appeals to a nostalgic view of childhood that may have existed for some, but certainly not across the world, nor over time. By setting up this idealised childhood, however, a childhood that is being 'eroded' and 'lost', the letter sets up 'good' and 'bad' childhood – and 'good' and 'bad' parenting. The letter seems to be as much about monitoring parental choices and behaviour as it is about policy change.

Conclusion

The concepts and theorisations about moral panics are illuminating. Combined with well-rehearsed analyses of how childhood is constructed, historically and more recently, they illuminate the letter's moral work: presenting nostalgic, idealised constructions of childhood that need protection. There is a good childhood – one that is outdoors and connected with nature, focusing on learning through play – and a bad childhood – one that is indoors and obsessed by screen-based technology, pressured by formal learning, tests and targets. The letter is less about children and more about childhood, and less about childhood than about parenthood, especially a category of parent that 'allows' a bad childhood. This analysis underlines the *productivity* of moral panics, the 'culture wars' referred to by Garland (2008), which in this letter redistribute social status between good and bad parents.

A close look at the letter's progression, from paragraph to paragraph, shows an initial appeal to expertise and research evidence, to rhetorical claims to know parental concerns, referring to our children, and placing itself as a grassroots movement in contrast to top-down, political approaches. This both fits and contrasts with the expertise and professionalism expressed within the signatories' identities. The very few claims among the signatories to be parents or grandparents highlight how these are *not* identities listed by most signatories. The moral entrepreneurship may have appealed to the collectivity of parents and grassroots support, but expertise – and even more so, *being* experts – was the strongest claim.

To consider this letter, concepts and theories of moral panic thus help to provide a fresh analysis of familiar ideas within debates about childhood. The lobbying work of a combination of experts and spokespeople, coupled with a particular moral standpoint, could certainly be regarded as claims-making activity and one of the features of the stages of a moral panic. However, Garland reminds us that describing an episode as a moral panic can be merely taking a different moral viewpoint from those who are alarmed. Garland goes further, writing about the 'ethics of attribution', where, empirically, a moral-panic analysis can be applied but 'ethical considerations make the attribution seem tactless, morally insensitive, or otherwise inappropriate' (Garland, 2008, p 24). There is every reason to think that the letter's organisers, and the signatories, were well intentioned, willing to put their energy, their professional standing and their commitment to influencing change. They used familiar tropes and rhetoric, tapping into what the media like to print and tell, which may have made it more likely that the letter would be printed and provided potential for further stories to be generated. If every initiative by civic society is characterised as a moral panic, then this undervalues and undermines people's public action and empties the term of meaning. Whether or not something contributes to a moral panic can often be judged only with the benefit of hindsight, and frequently it is the use to which such expressions are put, rather than the original expression of concern.

This chapter does not want to suggest that the letter, or others like it, are the expressions of, or stimulants to, fully fledged moral panics. They put forward particular ideas of childhood that are, arguably, ahistorical and idealised and convey notions of right and wrong in parenting, but they are seeking to galvanise change to a perceived better goal. The lens of moral panic illuminates the claims being made and the work being done within the text. But the possibility of discussion provides a constructive way forward, where we can look critically at knowledge claims and evidence and debate productively, involving parents, 'experts' – and children – to decide on future policy and practice.

Notes

[1] For example, see M. Narey (2007) '"Toxic childhood" harms British youth', *Telegraph* (13 September), www.telegraph.co.uk/news/uknews/1562980/Toxic-childhood-harms-British-youth.html (accessed 8.7.14); M. Easton (2009) 'Selfish adults "damage childhood"', BBC News (2 February), http://news.bbc.co.uk/1/hi/7861762.stm (accessed 8 July 2014); B. Fenton (2006) 'Junk culture "is poisoning our children"', *Telegraph* (12 September), www.telegraph.co.uk/news/1528642/Junk-culture-is-poisoning-our-children.html

(accessed 8 July 2014); Press Association (2014) 'Children's mental health menaced by "unprecedented toxic climate"', *Guardian* (20 January), www.theguardian.com/society/2014/jan/20/children-mental-health-toxic-climate-young-people (accessed 8 July 2014).

[2] Those who organised the letter, with others, moved to develop a group, Early Childhood Action, in February 2012, with the catchphrase on their website 'Fearlessly speaking professional truth to power'. See www.earlychildhoodaction.com/ (accessed 9 July 2014).

References

Buckingham, D. (2011) *The material child: Growing up in consumer culture*, Cambridge: Polity Press.

Clapton, G., Cree, V. and Smith, M. (2013) 'Moral panics, claims-making and child protection in the UK', *British Journal of Social Work*, vol 43, pp 803–12.

Cohen, S. (1972) *Folk devils and moral panics*, St Albans: Paladin.

Cornwall, A. and Brock, K. (2005) 'What do buzzwords do for development policy? A critical look at "participation", "empowerment" and "poverty reduction"', *Third World Quarterly*, vol 26, no 7, pp 1043–60.

Critcher, C. (2012) 'Moral panics and the media: ten years on', presentation at Seminar 1, Moral Panics Seminar Series, 23 September, Edinburgh: Edinburgh University, unpublished.

Cunningham, H. (2005) *Children and childhood in Western society since 1500*, Harlow: Pearson Longman.

Garland, D. (2008) 'On the concept of moral panic', *Crime Media Culture,* vol 4, no 9, pp 9–30.

Goode, E. (2012) 'The moral panic: dead or alive?', presentation at Seminar 1 Moral Panics Seminar Series, 23 September, Edinburgh: Edinburgh University.

Hendrick, H. (1997) 'Constructions and re-constructions of British childhood: an interpretive survey, 1800 to the present', in A. James and A. Prout (eds) *Constructing and reconstructing childhood* (2nd edn), London: Falmer.

Jackson, L. (2013) 'The case of the "good time girl": revisiting the postwar moral panic through the lens of gender', presentation at Seminar 2, Moral Panics Seminar Series, 17 May, Bath: Bath University, http://moralpanicseminars.wordpress.com/seminar-2/ (accessed 9 July 2014).

James, A. (2009) 'Agency', in J. Qvortrup, W.A. Corsaro and M. Honig (eds) *The Palgrave handbook of childhood studies*, Basingstoke: Palgrave, pp 34–45.

James, A., Jenks, C. and Prout, A. (1998) *Theorizing childhood*, Cambridge: Polity Press.

Jenkins, P. (1992) *Intimate enemies: Moral panics in contemporary Britain*, New York: Aldine de Gruyter.

Jenks, C. (1996) *Childhood*, Abingdon: Psychology Press.

McRobbie, A. and Thornton, S. (1995) 'Rethinking "moral panic" for multi-mediated social worlds', *British Journal of Sociology*, vol 46, no 4, pp 559–71.

Oswell, D. (2013) *The agency of children*, Cambridge: Cambridge University Press.

Qvortrup, J. (2009) 'Childhood as a structural form', in J. Qvortrup, W.A. Corsaro and M. Honig (eds) *The Palgrave handbook of childhood studies*, Basingstoke: Palgrave, Basingstoke: Palgrave, pp 21–33.

Teamey, K. and Hinton, R. (2014) 'Reflections on participation and its link with transformative processes', in E.K.M. Tisdall, A.M. Gadda and U.M. Butler (eds) *Children and young people's participation and its transformative potential*, Basingstoke: Palgrave, pp 22–43.

Telegraph (2011) 'Erosion of childhood' (23 September), www.telegraph.co.uk/education/educationnews/8784996/Erosion-of-childhood-letter-with-full-list-of-signatories.html (accessed 9 July 2014).

Tisdall, E.K.M. (2014) 'Children should be seen and heard? Children and young people's participation in the UK', in E.K.M. Tisdall, A.M. Gadda and U.M. Butler (eds) *Children and young people's participation and its transformative potential*, Basingstoke: Palgrave, pp 168–88.

UNICEF Innocenti Centre (2007) *Innocenti Report Card 7: Child poverty in perspective: An overview of child well-being in rich countries*, www.unicef-irc.org/publications/445 (accessed 9 July 2014).

Wells, K. (2009) *Childhood in a global perspective*, Cambridge: Polity Press.

Zelizer, V.A. (1985) *Pricing the priceless child: The changing social value of children*, Princeton, NJ: Princeton University Press.

FOUR

Internet risk research and child sexual abuse: a misdirected moral panic?

Ethel Quayle

The collision of recent technological change and fears about sexual risk to children has seemed to polarise debates about online activity by young people and those thought to have a sexual interest in children. Finkelhor (2014) describes the alarmism reflected by scholarly and journalistic literature, which is founded on assumptions about the amplification of deviance, the role and dynamics of the digital environment, and remedies to the problems lying in specialised internet education programmes. He also points out that research findings do not appear to support these assumptions. In many countries, particularly the United States, the rates of child sexual abuse show a decline (Laaksonen et al, 2011; Radford et al, 2011; Finkelhor and Jones, 2012), and only a small proportion of sexual offences against children in the US have an online component (Wolak, Finkelhor and Mitchell, 2009). Bullying, as a form of peer-related aggression, still shows higher rates in face-to-face as opposed to online activity (Livingstone et al, 2011). The US research would also indicate that most online offenders are people who know their victims from offline contexts, and the dynamics of online and offline offenders are similar (Wolak and Finkelhor, 2013), although in the latter analysis the sample reflected two groups that used online communication for sexual communication with a minor. One group was known to the young person in the offline world (family or acquaintances) and the other had first met the young person online, although both used the internet or mobile phone to engage sexually with a minor. In his paper, which was written as a response to Livingstone and Smith (2014), Finkelhor lists many of the positive ways in which technology has facilitated the social development of children, has potentially kept them safe and has provided a buffer to possible harmful risk taking and suggests that it may warrant further exploration 'once the scholarly imagination moves beyond the techno-panic mind set' (Finkelhor, 2014, p 656).

Others have also reminded us that problems such as bullying are serious, and in some cases can lead to suicide, but that this is a serious social problem rather than a technical one (Berg and Breheny, 2014). These authors also note that there have been similar panics in relation to the detrimental effects of subliminal messaging, comic books, cyber pornography and video games on the well-being and behaviour of young people. These concerns do not appear to relate to the demonising of technology per se, but to the fact that in Australia anxieties about harms against children were going to result in a Children's e-Safety Commissioner, with powers to take down material from social media websites, which would represent an increase in government control over the internet and potentially threaten free speech. Other concerns about the impact of technology on the behaviour of young people include fears of ICT-enhanced plagiarism among students (Trushell and Byrne, 2013), as well as companies exploiting a legal loophole to promote unhealthy food and drink consumption through the use of online games (advergames) that include advertisements (www.bbc. co.uk/news/uk-27647445).

Moral panics are generally conceived as a disproportionate public reaction to an event or group that poses a threat to the moral order (Cohen, 1972). The public's fear and unease about the risk of sexual offending against children, and law-enforcement response (or at times a perceived lack of response), have been evident since the 1950s and clearly remain so today. Similarly to the arguments put forward by Finkelhor (2014), it has been suggested that behind all of these constructions there are 'extra-scientific pressures' rather than 'pristine objective reality' (Jenkins, 1998), and that the most recent panics over sex offenders are the consequence of a culture that disproportionately emphasises child protection – and are likely to remain so because of the establishment of the child-welfare movement, health and mental health services and the increased involvement of women in decision making (Fox, 2013). Jenkins (1998) argued that social change has been reinforced by the institutionalisation of the 'child-protection idea' (Jenkins, 1998, p 233) such that it would be unthinkable that any government could seek to return to the status quo of the 1950s or 1960s without facing allegations of 'being soft on child molestation'. Equally, the democratisation of psychiatric and psychological therapies has not only increased access to services but, as suggested by Jenkins (1998), has produced 'a huge constituency with an overwhelming interest in keeping these issues at the center of public concern' (Jenkins, 1998, p 233). Jewkes (2010) suggested that anxieties about crime and safety, and an aversion to risk, have led to a form of social retreat (evidenced in the market for secure housing developments, gated communities, four-wheel-drive vehicles) and that this has resulted, for children and young people, in the denial of freedoms previously enjoyed by their parents. However, paradoxically, the internet is also a form of social retreat, yet potentially provides a freedom of thought, expression and identity presentation unlike anything that young people may have at their disposal in the offline environment. These apparent freedoms may be perceived as a threat to parents' ability to manage their children, particularly in relation to sexual risk taking.

However, Jewkes (2010) has argued that the reason why media stories about child sexual abuse and the internet occupy such a unique place in the collective 'psyche' is because sex, risk and children are three of the twelve cardinal news values that shape news production in the 21st century. This would appear to situate much of the current anxiety about the dangers of the internet for young people in a more overarching anxiety about children and sexual abuse. In the United Kingdom, the last few years have seen a preoccupation with historical and current sexual abuse cases, an obvious example being Operation Yewtree, launched by the police in the wake of the allegations against Jimmy Savile. These stories dominate the popular media and, as suggested by Jewkes, convey the behaviour of adults who are sexually attracted to children and adolescents in extremely negative terms and ignore the complexities of adult–child relations. She argues that constituting the paedophile as the number one folk devil sits oddly with a society that, in areas such as fashion, beauty and art, seeks to fetishise and market youthful bodies. Papadopoulos (2010), author of the Home Office's *Sexualisation of Young People Review* for the British government, presents arguments about the sexualisation of youth that suggest that there is increasing exposure to hyper-sexualised images and that children and young people are also pressured into looking 'sexy' and 'hot'. However, Egan and Hawkes (2012) have argued that the current discourse on sexualisation draws on and reproduces many of the same deeply problematic assumptions regarding the child and its sexuality as purity advocates did over a century ago.

The preoccupation with innocent children and dangerous adults (peer violence outside of bullying does not seem to attract as much attention) sits alongside our excitement and intoxication with the changes brought about by rapid technological development. We are still concerned with sexual abuse, but in some ways (as with celebrity offenders) the internet allows us to position it elsewhere, reinforcing the construction of the dangerous stranger (Jewkes and Wykes, 2012). Ost (2002) suggested a similar moral panic in terms of the threat that child pornography, and those who possess it, is thought to pose to society. As society attempts to tackle the problems of child sexual abuse, tracking down those who possess indecent images of children may be seen as a more attainable goal than eradicating child sexual abuse that may manifest itself in peer circles known to the child or in the family home. Indeed, it may be the very success of law enforcement in successfully arresting those who commit technology-mediated crimes against children that reinforces the likelihood of future investment in this area by both law-enforcement agencies and those who drive policies and legislation. An example from the US of undercover online police operations indicated that interviews with law enforcement about a nationally representative sample of cases ending in arrest for an internet-related sex crime against a minor in 2000 and 2006 suggested a 280% increase in arrests of offenders between the two time periods. The estimated numbers of arrests nationwide grew from 826 to 3,137 (Mitchell et al, 2010).

The success of law enforcement is also mirrored in the increasing number of convictions for possession of indecent images of children (Wolak et al, 2011), which may be a result of higher levels of activity by law enforcement or may reflect a migration of some sexual offending to the online environment. The success of these cases may also relate to the fact that these crimes, unlike many other sexual crimes against children, leave a permanent product in the form of images or texts, which provide clear evidence of a crime's having been committed.

Our concerns about the risks posed by technological change mean that there has been considerable interest in two areas of academic research. The first has examined the similarities and differences between online offenders and contact offenders, and the likelihood of those who possess indecent images of children either having already committed or going on to commit contact offences against children. The second has focused on the vulnerabilities of young people online, and has also led to debates about the prevalence of 'sexting' (sending or receiving sexually explicit images and texts) and its psychological correlates, the majority of them negative (Klettke, Hallford and Mellor, 2014). Only a few voices have argued for a normalcy discourse, suggesting the need for an evidence-based approach to sexting risk prevention that acknowledges both adolescent vulnerability and sexual agency (Döring, 2014). There has been very little interest, outside of victim-identification units within law enforcement, in the children who appear in these indecent images (for example, Svedin and Back, 2003; Quayle and Jones, 2011; Jonsson and Svedin, 2012), other than what they might tell us about the offender (Osborn, Elliott and Beech, 2010; Seto, Reeves and Jung, 2010). Jenkins (2009) asked the question as to why the issue of child pornography has failed to generate a panic when it appears to fulfil the classic criteria. He suggests that moral-panic theory was founded on a set of implicit value judgements that assumed that the topic under discussion must by definition be bogus or exaggerated. Jenkins argues that 'The understanding of social problems must rely primarily on analysing the rhetorical work of claims-makers and their ability (or lack of it) to appeal to public tastes and prejudices, which may or may not be well founded' (Jenkins, 2009, p 36) and that child pornography offers one instance where there has been a surprising lack of panic. From his own research observing internet bulletin board traffic related to those both using and producing indecent images, he had earlier claimed that the trade in images is considerably greater than had been acknowledged (Jenkins, 2001). This would certainly resonate with the views of many people in law enforcement, although the reality is that we have really no strong basis on which to judge the size of the problem, outside of the databases of known images held by law enforcement. It is difficult to confirm whether the trade in indecent images has increased with the advent of the internet, although one pre-internet study by Schuijer and Rossen (1992) would suggest that at the time of the study the numbers involved in both image production and image use were much smaller, as were the number of children exploited. Jenkins also suggested that many of these images are new or recent and therefore depict the on-going sexual abuse or exploitation of children. His argument of grounds for a moral panic is that the underlying situation is large scale and could easily be portrayed as threatening, particularly because children are central to the problem. It also appears to be an expanding problem (it is difficult for it to be a contracting problem, given that it is a challenge to remove content once it has been widely distributed) and it is certainly global, in that the internet has no obvious geographical boundaries. Jenkins argues that the issue of indecent images also brings in the harmful effects of globalisation, the undermining of national laws and sovereignty, and offers all kinds of additional issues including popular fears about technology and the exploitation of children by sinister men: 'And the demon figures are ready and waiting' (Jenkins, 2001, p 38).

Jenkins (2009) accounts for the lack of moral panic because of the general lack of technical understanding on the part of many people in law enforcement, resulting in an annexing of the problem to the already known issues of child abuse. In addition, there is comprehensive official control of the issue and, as Mirkin (2009) has indicated, access to these images for the purpose of research is problematic, and this may have limited study of this area. There appear to be much bigger concerns about children being exposed to sexual content (for example,

Flood, 2009) rather than appearing in images of their abuse. One possibility is that the moral panic that exists in relation to technology and sexual risk has become tangential to sexual abuse with and through the production of indecent images. The majority of people will never have been exposed to such images, and Cooper (2011) has argued that even specialist medical professionals tasked with the care of children have shown a reluctance to engage with law enforcement in the examination of these cases. She suggests that this reluctance relates to many possible factors such as: feelings of aversion to the images; a disbelief that these represent real children; the difficulties of establishing a professional relationship with the images; a failure to appreciate that they represent a crime scene; and the lack of guidelines concerning the procedures for examining such material. The unease expressed in this assessment is mirrored in an observed discomfort on the part of, for example, the judiciary to examine the images related to prosecution cases. While there are strong ethical grounds for limiting access to these images, the result is that for most of us they remain unknown and unknowable. Our gaze is then drawn to those convicted of their possession, and the language used by popular media to describe the 'horrific' collections seized by the police (Travis, 2014) or even the possibility that our children might be exposed to them, while there is much less attention paid to the children depicted in them. The internet is therefore positioned as a place where predators wait to share images of abuse and, more saliently for most people, to catch our children when they are online. Perhaps what fuels these anxieties is the rapid expansion of technology in our everyday lives, with the competitive gallop of companies to produce not just phones but a range of connected devices, from home appliances to door locks and watches, that are able to communicate with each other (*Taipei Times*, 2014). Atzori, Iera and Morabito (2014) discuss the next development in this 'Internet of Things', which will include social-like capabilities that allow a network to enhance the level of trust between objects that are 'friends' with each other. At one level we are excited by these developments that quickly become embedded in routine activities, such as searching for information, buying tickets, paying bills and expanding our social networks. At another level, we imbue this technology with destructive power and fear for the safety (and control) of our children (Altobelli, 2010) in the face of those who use the internet as a playground for sexual perversion. Lim (2013) points out that the internet is neither a technology of hope nor a weapon of moral destruction; rather, the social impacts of the internet result from an organic interaction between technology and existing social, political and cultural structures. There are consequences to problematising the impact of technological change on the well-being and sexuality of young people. It potentially diverts attention away from the possibilities of technology as protective, providing a forum for risk taking that potentially has fewer consequences (Finkelhor, 2014), and instead results in considerable investment in protective strategies that may have little impact on the behaviour of young people (Mitchell et al, 2010). It may also lead to a diversion of resources away from service provision for children who have been sexually abused, along with less attention being paid to resourcing the identification of children in indecent images, which has not appeared to capture the public imagination or to have produced a claims maker to champion their cause.

References

Altobelli, T. (2010) 'Cyber-abuse – a new worldwide threat to children's rights', *Family Court Review*, vol 48, no 3, pp 459–81.

Atzori, L., Iera, A. and Morabito, G. (2014) 'From "smart objects" to "social objects": the next evolutionary step of the internet of things', *IEEE Communications Magazine*, vol 52, no 1, pp 97–105.

Berg, C. and Breheny, S. (2014) 'The cyberbullying moral panic', *IPA Review*, vol 66, no 1, pp 24–7.

Cohen, S. (1972) *Folk devils and moral panics: The creation of the Mods and Rockers*, London: McGibbon & Kee.

Cooper, S.W. (2011) 'The medical analysis of child sexual abuse images', *Journal of Child Sexual Abuse*, vol 20, no 6, pp 631–42.

Döring, N. (2014) 'Consensual sexting among adolescents: risk prevention through abstinence education or safer sexting?', *Cyberpsychology*, vol 8, no 1, pp 1–18.

Egan, R. and Hawkes, G. (2012) 'Sexuality, youth and the perils of endangered innocence: how history can help us get past the panic', *Gender & Education*, vol 24, no 3, pp 269–84.

Finkelhor, D. (2014) 'Commentary: cause for alarm? Youth and internet risk research – a commentary on Livingstone and Smith (2014)', *Journal of Child Psychology and Psychiatry*, vol 55, no 6, pp 655–8.

Finkelhor, D. and Jones, L.M. (2012) *Have sexual abuse and physical abuse declined since the 1990s?*, Durham, NH: Crimes against Children Research Center, University of New Hampshire.

Flood, M. (2009) 'The harms of pornography exposure among children and young people', *Child Abuse Review*, vol 18, no 6, pp 384–400.

Fox, K.J. (2013) 'Incurable sex offenders, lousy judges and the media: moral panic sustenance in the age of new media', *American Journal of Criminal Justice*, vol 38, pp 160–81.

Jenkins, P. (1998) *Moral panic: Changing concepts of the child molester in modern America*, New Haven, CT: Yale University Press.

Jenkins, P. (2001) *Beyond tolerance: Child pornography on the internet*, New York: New York University Press.

Jenkins, P. (2009) 'Failure to launch: why do some social issues fail to detonate moral panics?' *British Journal of Criminology*, vol 49, pp 35–47.

Jewkes, Y. (2010) 'Much ado about nothing? Representations and realities of online soliciting of children', *Journal of Sexual Aggression*, vol 16, no 1, pp 5–18.

Jewkes, Y. and Wykes, M. (2012) 'Reconstructing the sexual abuse of children: "cyber-paeds", panic and power', *Sexualities*, vol 15, no 8, pp 943–52.

Jonsson, L. and Svedin, C.G. (2012) 'Children within the images', in E. Quayle and K. Ribsil (eds) *Internet child pornography: Understanding and preventing on-line child abuse*, London: Routledge.

Klettke, B., Hallford, D.J. and Mellor, D.J. (2014) 'Sexting prevalence and correlates: A systematic literature review', *Clinical Psychology Review*, vol 34, pp 44–53.

Laaksonen, T., Sariola, H., Johansson, A., Jern, P., Varjonen, M., Von Der Pahlen, B. and Santtila, P. (2011) 'Changes in the prevalence of child sexual abuse, its risk factors, and their associations as a function of age cohort in a Finnish population sample', *Child Abuse & Neglect*, vol 35, no 7, pp 480–90.

Lim, M. (2013) 'The internet and everyday life in Indonesia: A new moral panic?', *Bijdragen tot de Tall-, Land-en Volkenkunde*, vol 169, pp 133–47.

Livingstone, S. and Smith, P.K. (2014) 'Annual research review: harms experienced by child users of online and mobile technologies: the nature, prevalence and management of sexual and aggressive risks in the digital age', *Journal of Child Psychology and Psychiatry*, vol 55, pp 635–54.

Livingstone, S., Haddon, L., Gorzig, A. and Olafsson, K. (2011) *Risks and safety on the internet: The perspective of European children: full findings*, London: LSE, EU Kids Online, http://eprints.lse.ac.uk/33731/.

Mirkin, H. (2009) 'The social, political, and legal construction of the concept of child pornography', *Journal of Homosexuality*, vol 56, pp 233–67.

Mitchell, K., Finkelhor, D., Jones, L. and Wolak, J. (2010) 'Growth and change in undercover online child exploitation investigations, 2000–2006', *Policing & Society*, vol 20, no 4, pp 416–31.

Osborn, J., Elliott, I.A. and Beech, A.R. (2010) 'The use of actuarial risk assessment measures with UK internet child pornography offenders', *Journal of Aggression, Conflict and Peace Research*, vol 2, no 3, pp 16–24.

Ost, S. (2002). 'Children at risk: legal and societal perceptions of the potential threat that the possession of child pornography poses for society', *Journal of Law and Society,* vol 29, no 3, pp 436–60.

Papadopoulos, L. (2010) *Sexualisation of Young People Review*, London: Home Office.

Quayle, E. and Jones, T. (2011) 'Sexualized images of children on the internet', *Sexual Abuse: A Journal of Research & Treatment*, vol 23, no 1, pp 7–21.

Radford, L., Corral, S., Bradley, C., Fisher, H., Basset, C., Howat, N. and Collishaw, S. (2011) *Child abuse and neglect in the UK today*, London: NSPCC.

Schuijer, J. and Rossen, B. (1992) 'The trade in child pornography', *IPT forensics*, 4, cited in Y. Jewkes and M. Yar (eds) *The handbook of internet crime*, Cullompton: Willan.

Seto, M.C., Reeves, L. and Jung, S. (2010) 'Motives for child pornography offending: The explanations given by the offenders', *Journal of Sexual Aggression*, vol 16, pp 169–80.

Svedin, C.G. and Back, K. (2003) *Why didn't they tell us? Sexual abuse in child pornography*, Stockholm: Save the Children Sweden.

Taipei Times (2014) 'Samsung unwraps Tizen for "Internet of Things"', www.taipeitimes.com/News/biz/archives/2014/06/05/2003592005 (accessed 24 July 2014).

Travis, A. (2014) 'Online child abuse images becoming "more extreme, sadistic and violent"', *Guardian* (11 March), www.theguardian.com/society/2014/mar/11/online-child-abuse-images-more-extreme-sadistic-violent.

Trushell, J. and Byrne, K. (2013) 'Education undergraduates and ICT-enhanced academic dishonesty: A moral panic?', *British Journal of Educational Technology,* vol 44, no 1, pp 6–19.

Wolak, J. and Finkelhor, D. (2013) 'Are crimes by online predators different from crimes by sex offenders who know youth in-person?', *The Journal of Adolescent Health*, vol 53, pp 736–41.

Wolak, J., Finkelhor, D. and Mitchell, K.J. (2009) *Trends in arrests of 'online predators'*, Durham, NH: Crimes against Children Research Center, University of New Hampshire.

Wolak, J., Finkelhor, D., Mitchell, K. and Jones, L. (2011) 'Arrests for child pornography production: data at two time points from a national sample of U.S. law enforcement agencies', *Child Maltreatment*, vol 16, no 3, pp 184–95.

FIVE

The Rotherham abuse scandal

Anneke Meyer

Introduction

This chapter examines the Rotherham abuse scandal, which centres on the exploitation and abuse of (mostly) teenage girls between 1997 and 2013 in the South Yorkshire town of Rotherham and the publication of an official inquiry report (Jay, 2014) into the abuse and, more specifically, into agencies' response to it. The report was released on 26 August 2014 and sparked intense media coverage. It is not difficult to see why. The report details the violent and sexual abuse and trafficking of minors, often over a number of years, carried out by groups of men who had befriended these children 'on the streets'. This pattern of abuse is described as 'child sexual exploitation' (CSE). The report identifies 1,400 victims, emphasising that this is a 'conservative estimate'. Around a third were in local council care or known to social services. The report is highly critical of the two key agencies in charge of CSE, namely the police and the council and its social and children's services. It paints a picture of serious failings and repeated inaction; Jay particularly criticises senior staff and management who actively ignored concerns about CSE.

This chapter considers the Rotherham abuse scandal from a moral panic perspective. It explores in detail media representations of the scale of the problem and the framing of blame, two key elements through which moral panics are instigated (Cohen, 2002). To this end, a limited press analysis was carried out in which the coverage of four newspapers was examined during the five days following the release of the Jay report. The newspapers were chosen to capture opposite ends of the political spectrum and the market: the legalist and moderately conservative broadsheet, *The Times*; the populist conservative tabloid, the *Sun*; the staunchly and morally conservative, mid-market paper, the *Daily Mail*; and the liberal left-wing broadsheet, the *Guardian*. A search of the LexisLibrary database produced a total of 180 articles for the time-period, between 30 and 38 per day, confirming that this was indeed a scandal of considerable proportion.

The Rotherham abuse scandal and moral panic theory

The nature and scale of the problem

In his analysis of moral panics Cohen (2002) argues that heightened societal interest and outrage are driven by media representations of the subject as a serious and large-scale problem, indicative of the moral malaise of society as a whole. Strategies for creating this picture include the use of emotive and moralistic language, sensational and alarming claims, distortion and exaggeration, prediction and symbolisation.

Newspaper reporting of the Rotherham scandal demonstrates this clearly, and labelling is key to this. Jay (2014) defines what happened in Rotherham as 'CSE', although what is meant by this term is not always clear, either in the report or in the wider coverage, perhaps not surprisingly, since the term is a relatively recent invention to include both child sexual abuse and child trafficking (Cree et al, 2014). In spite of the lack of clarity about the label CSE, the abuse itself is graphically described, in both the report and in the newspapers that covered it; and in each case the specific scandal around CSE in Rotherham is turned into a nationwide problem. For example, the scale of CSE is described as 'endemic' (*Guardian*, 28 August); 'grooming' is presented as at a 'Horrific scale' (*Daily Mail*, 31 August); and Rotherham is only the tip of the iceberg, as the 'same abuse is continuing to happen across the country' (*Guardian*, 28 August). The *Daily Mail* predicts that the problem is increasing, describing is as 'overwhelming' and growing 'out of control' (31 August) and claims in prominent headlines that 'THE ABUSE IS STILL GOING ON – AND NOW IT'S EVEN

WORSE' (27 August). Meanwhile, the *Guardian's* editorial (28 August) asserts that hard evidence is no longer needed because, 'Absence of evidence is not evidence of absence, and a pattern of abuse that has now resulted in convictions in towns from Torbay to Rochdale is very likely to be happening in other places not yet identified.' The scandal itself is seen as indicative of a wider moral malaise in which society has become so brutal and amoral that something like this could occur: 'HOW CAN THIS HAPPEN IN A CIVILISED COUNTRY?' the *Daily Mail* (27 August) asks.

All newspapers prominently and repeatedly refer to the official figure of 1,400 victims. There is no critical analysis of this figure. Moreover, the media sensationalises the number through emotive language and front-page headlines such as '1400 lost girls' (*The Times*, 27 August). And the net is cast widely to include even potential victims: '[A]n extensive report into the nature of child sexual exploitation [...] estimated that 16,500 children were at risk of a specific type of abuse that can see gangs of abusers grooming children as young as 11' (*Guardian*, 28 August).

The scale of CSE is further constructed through the theme of nationwide 'grooming gangs'. Three out of the four newspapers (*The Times*, the *Daily Mail* and the *Sun*) focus on the issue of organised groups of Asian men who systematically befriend, exploit and abuse white teenage girls. A wide range of shorthands is used to refer to this phenomenon, either with or without an ethnic prefix: for example, '(Asian) grooming gangs'; '(Asian) sex gangs'; '(Asian) grooming networks'; 'groups of Asian (or Pakistani) men grooming'; 'Asian (or Pakistani) gangs' and so on. This over-wording indicates preoccupation (Fairclough, 1989) and because 'sex gangs' are reported to be active in towns across the UK – the most commonly cited examples including Rochdale, Oxford, Derby and Telford (*Daily Mail*, 27 August; *Sun*, 31 August) – the Rotherham scandal is turned into a nationwide problem. *The Times* also gives a sense of these networks being a significant problem across Britain, particularly the North of England and the Midlands (28 August), but this is not reported with any sense of panic. In contrast, the *Sun* and the *Daily Mail* are much more alarmist. Sex gangs are represented as a problem of huge proportions. The *Sun* features headlines such as 'ABUSE GANGS UK; CHILD SEX SCANDAL POLICE TO REOPEN 1,000 MORE FILES' and claims that an 'industrial scale gang-rape and trafficking of children' exists; 'similar large-scale exploitation of young girls by gangs is happening right across the UK' (31 August). The *Sun* meanwhile demands a nationwide inquiry and urges readers to sign a petition for this (31 August).

Blame, folk devils and the issue of ethnicity

Blame is an essential part of moral panics, as culprits are demonised to the extent of becoming folk devils. The culprits are usually the perpetrators of deviance, but many moral panics around child abuse have also demonised social workers for failing to protect children in their care (for example, Franklin and Parton, 1991; Critcher, 2003). In the Rotherham abuse scandal, the focus is on the public sector system and its failings, as well as on Asian men.

All four newspapers are highly critical of the authorities in charge of CSE in Rotherham, notably Rotherham council, with its social services, and South Yorkshire police. The two broadsheets describe in detail the authorities' failure to act and term errors 'blatant' and 'catastrophic'. There is a moralistic theme of lack of response amounting to the 'betrayal of children', which renders the authorities callous. An editorial in *The Times* (28 August) writes that victims 'were not just tortured by criminals but betrayed by child protection professionals and ridiculed by police', while the *Guardian* judges that the authorities in Rotherham were responsible for 'the most shameful mass betrayal of young people in the history of children's safeguarding' (27 August). The *Times* also personalises blame by sensationally labelling staff a 'disgrace' and 'as bad as the perpetrators' (28 August). However, large parts of the broadsheet coverage are neutral in tone and fact based. For example, both *The Times* and the *Guardian* make a distinction between senior managers and front-line staff. In line with

Jay's (2014) report, they accuse senior figures in the council and the police of systematically ignoring knowledge of CSE.

The *Daily Mail* and the *Sun* are far more emotive and sensational in their critique of the authorities. The *Sun* criticises Rotherham council for a 'sickening dereliction of duty towards 1,400 victims of paedophile rape' and says about the police that 'their incompetence and callousness towards these children simply boggles the mind' (28 August). The editorial the previous day describes the failure to act as a deliberate, calculated strategy:

> They knew about it for years. But the Left-wing council let it go on because the rapists were Asian. Senior officials ordered worried staff to downplay it for fear of being accused of racism. Think about that. They prioritised political correctness over the gang-rape of children. [...] The council and police did nothing. But not through oversight or incompetence. This was policy. (*Sun*, 27 August)

This quotation thus renders senior council staff as truly inhuman, because they did not care about the suffering of children. But more than this, they chose to protect themselves from accusations of racism. Racism and ethnicity shape the dynamics of blame in the Rotherham scandal; this issue has been given so much media attention as to become synonymous with the scandal itself. The *Sun* and the *Daily Mail* shape this discourse into an attack on what they pejoratively term 'PC culture'. They argue that left-wing politics dominate local government and create a climate of political correctness in which 'the truth' cannot be spoken. The blame, then, is laid less with individual social workers and more with a way of thinking, demonised on front-page headlines such as the *Sun*'s '1,400 VICTIMS OF PC BRIGADE; CHILDREN ABUSED FOR 16YRS' and its editorial, 'Left's blind eye to child rapes' (27 August). The first *Daily Mail* editorial on the scandal also identifies 'PC culture' as the culprit:

But perhaps most chilling is the reason why so many officials were reluctant to get to the bottom of these vile crimes. [...] Several staff described being nervous about identifying the ethnic origins of perpetrators for fear of being thought 'racist'; others remembered clear directions from managers not to do so. [...] The inescapable conclusion is that the dictates of political correctness were placed above the duty to protect children against violent abuse. (*Daily Mail*, 27 August)

The essence is that this culture is 'letting evil thrive' (*Daily Mail*, 28 August), rendering it guilty and evil by implication. As the scandal is seen as indicative of a wider moral malaise, 'PC culture' becomes responsible for the lack of decency, virtue and morality that blights contemporary society. Yet Jay's (2014) report concludes that a complex puzzle of many contributory factors led to authorities' reluctance to act; focusing only on 'PC culture' ignores the wider context in which agencies were operating and misrepresents Jay's conclusion. Furthermore, when the 'PC culture' argument is linked to multiculturalism and the ethnic and religious backgrounds of perpetrators, the *Daily Mail* and the *Sun* become racist. A lack of morality is identified as the cause of CSE: only evil people could have perpetrated such horrific crimes. This lack of morality is not limited to specific perpetrators but attributed to the entire Asian and Muslim community. The *Sun* states in an article headlined 'ANYONE who thinks the Rotherham sex abuse was not about race is kidding themselves':

British Pakistani Muslims saw white children as trash. And now there should be a million British Muslims marching in the street saying – not in our name. [...] When some new controversy surrounds British Muslims we always hear about the 'overwhelming majority' of British Muslims who are proud to share British values. Why do we never see them? (*Sun*, 31 August)

The final question insinuates that it is a myth that most Muslims subscribe to British values, meaning that they have either different values or none at all. Given the context – the Rotherham scandal, the Asian background of offenders, their supposed hatred of white children and a headline that tells readers that 'race' was a causal factor – the logical conclusion is set up for readers that this lack of British (read 'proper') values in the Asian Muslim community is the cause of CSE (Fairclough, 1989). This then becomes an attack on multiculturalism:

> [T]his show[s] the terrible damage done by the ideology of multiculturalism which, in Rotherham, was elevated above the requirements of law enforcement and compassionate morality. [...] Thanks to this dogma, we no longer have a universal moral code or national identity, and the consequences can be seen all around us, whether in the rise of home-grown Islamic extremism or in the failure of too many migrant groups to learn even basic English. The advance of multiculturalism across our civic life has been fuelled by the deepening official fixation with anti-racism. (*Daily Mail*, 28 August)

The problem with multiculturalism is thus its refusal to enforce the British moral code on all ethnic groups. Of course, neither the *Sun* nor the *Daily Mail* says this directly, but they strongly cue their readers into these conclusions as the only logical ones (Fairclough, 1989). In contrast, the two broadsheets mention a number of causal factors highlighted by the Jay report, including poverty, budget cuts, gender and class issues. As a consequence, even when *The Times* highlights the 'fear of being labelled as racist' argument, this does not appear as a stand-alone explanation. The *Guardian* likewise emphasises that members of all ethnic groups carry out CSE (28 August) and, with *The Times* (30 August), voices the opinion that the social class of the victims, rather than ethnicity of the perpetrators, was the main reason for authority inaction. Both newspapers point to statistics indicating that the vast majority of sex offenders are white males.

Discussion and conclusion: the Rotherham scandal, the media and social work

All newspapers' treatment of the issue demonstrates the 'politics of outrage' that routinely accompanies child-protection controversies (Parton, 2014): they portray Rotherham as a scandal, agree that CSE is a serious and widespread problem, share common themes such as authority failure and use dramatic language. But considerable differences were found between the newspapers, attributable to market category and political orientation. The two broadsheets used more factual language, provided significantly more information, and were therefore less simplistic and more accurate. Given this diversity and complexity of newspaper positions, it is impossible to identify the kind of media consensus Cohen envisages as occurring during a moral panic. This is especially true for the issue of blame.

Franklin and Parton (1991) note that moral panic theory has never been able to fully explain why, in cases of child abuse, the media do not turn on the perpetrators, the obvious 'folk devils', but instead blame social workers. In the Rotherham scandal, social services are frequently criticised, but this does not turn into the full-blown social worker demonisation typical of other child-abuse cases (Critcher, 2003). This is despite the case's possessing all the necessary ingredients, such as children being abused, many victims being known to social services and abuse not being detected or successfully dealt with for years. Aldridge (1999) argues that this is due to social work's diminished significance as a political symbol; however, the vilification of social work during the high-profile 'Baby P' case in 2007–08 clearly undermines this idea (Parton, 2014). Rather, it appears that social workers did not feature as folk devils in the Rotherham scandal because of several interacting factors, namely newspaper politics, the Jay report, the nature of the case and the sensitivity of the topic of ethnicity.

The two most sensational newspapers in the study, the *Sun* and the *Daily Mail*, turned their anger on 'PC culture', which shifted the focus away from social work per se. The two papers blamed a wider culture that they suspect to dominate the entire public sector. In the early 1990s, Franklin and Parton wrote that social workers are often presented in the media as a 'symbol for the entire public sector, personifying "evil" which the political new right presumes to be inherent therein' (Franklin and Parton, 1991, p 9). In the Rotherham case, right-wing newspapers like the *Sun* and the *Daily Mail* used 'PC culture' rather than social work as a metaphor to wage war on the public sector they detest. The focus on 'PC culture' may be grounded in Jay's (2014) report, which identifies that front-line workers (social workers, youth workers) repeatedly tried to raise awareness with senior officials, who failed to act. In the light of this, stereotyping social workers as soft, ineffectual, ignorant and uncaring (Franklin and Parton, 1991) would have required quite a discursive sleight of hand. The serial nature of child-protection scandals means that, over time, certain discourses are entrenched and come to serve as ready-made interpretive frameworks for further scandals; the explanatory discourse of 'institutional failure' is a particularly important one (Parton, 2014). Child abuse is always the domain of the police as well as social services, but the media tend to focus on and blame social services (Franklin and Parton, 1991). Arguably, the type of abuse at the centre of the Rotherham scandal was so obviously criminal that it was difficult for the media to ignore the role of the police. As a consequence, the discourse of 'institutional failure' had to be applied to the police and any full-blown vilification of the authorities would have had to focus on the police as well as social services. This may have contributed to the reluctance of conservative papers to engage in outright demonisation, because they tend to be supportive of the police, whom they see as maintaining law and order on behalf of the moral majority.

In the end, no single folk devil emerges in the Rotherham scandal. A vague entity such as 'PC culture' does not lend itself to demonisation, as labels of evil are difficult to attach in a meaningful way. Asian men forming 'sex gangs' were obvious folk-devil candidates, but the *Guardian* does not support the theme and *The Times* is rather reluctant, despite its conservative leaning, possibly because of the sensitivity of the issue of ethnicity. As a consequence, the blame game is marked by complexity and diversity. A moral-panic lens helps to illuminate the media treatment of the Rotherham scandal, allowing insights into the framing of CSE as a national problem through distorted claims and emotive language, but it may overestimate consensus, and so cannot fully capture the discursive complexity of the case.

References

Aldridge, M. (1999) 'Poor relations: state social work and the press in the UK', in B. Franklin (ed) *Social policy, the media and misrepresentation*, London: Routledge, pp 89–103.

Cohen, S. (2002) *Folk devils and moral panics: The creation of the Mods and Rockers* (3rd edn), London and New York: Routledge.

Cree, V.E., Clapton, G. and Smith, M. (2014) 'The presentation of child trafficking in the UK: an old and new moral panic?', *British Journal of Social Work*, vol 44, pp 418–33.

Critcher, C. (2003) *Moral panics and the media*, Milton Keynes: Open University Press.

Fairclough, N. (1989) *Language and power*, Harlow: Longman.

Franklin, B. and Parton, N. (1991) 'Media reporting of social work: a framework for analysis', in B. Franklin and N. Parton (eds) *Social work, the media and public relations*, London: Routledge.

Jay, A. (2014) *Independent inquiry into child sexual exploitation in Rotherham (1997–2013)*, Rotherham: Rotherham Metropolitan Borough Council.

Parton, N. (2014) *The politics of child protection: Contemporary developments and future directions*, Basingstoke: Palgrave Macmillan.

Afterword

Mark Hardy

Endings are commonplace within life and work and yet can often be neglected among the demands of front-line social work practice. There can be pressure to close cases once acute risks have been addressed. A difficult meeting or phone call is still on your mind in the evening or over the weekend. Ideally, an ending supports the transition between one state and another and often this is best achieved when it is prepared for in advance. While reading this book, you may have been thinking of your own work and asking yourself what difference an understanding of moral panics might make to your research, study or practice. Within this afterword, I hope to help in this transition from theory to practice by identifying what I feel are some of the key themes addressed by the contributors and discussing their relevance to the current context of social work policy and practice.

I am employed as a social worker in a local authority Children and Families practice team in Scotland and have previous experience of youth work and residential childcare. My current role encompasses child protection, children in need, looked after and accommodated children, and adoption and permanency work. This places my perspective within a specific context. Scotland has its own legal system and distinctive Children's Hearing System (see Hothersall, 2014). However, many of the issues facing social workers in Scotland have much in common with other child welfare systems in Anglophone countries (Lonne et al, 2009). I would like to concentrate on two broad themes, both of which are indicated in the quote from Stanley Cohen (1972) at the beginning of Chapter One by Ian Butler, and which in my opinion are particularly relevant for social work policy and practice: firstly, the way in which social problems are represented in moral panics; and secondly, the responses to those social problems.

Each of the contributions in this byte describes how a phenomenon, individual or group becomes defined as a social problem and represented through the media, politicians and other 'claims makers', or 'moral entrepreneurs', in ways that are over-simplified, stereotyped and distorted. Specific strategies are used by claims makers to foreground their opinions and construct problems according to particular ideologies. In Chapter Three Kay Tisdall uses the example of the 'lost childhood' trope and a letter printed in the media to show how claims makers represent themselves as holding relevant expertise and appeal to idealised constructions of childhood that construct good/bad dichotomies of childhood and parenting. Similar characterisations are described by Ethel Quayle in Chapter Four in relation to 'innocent children' and the dangers of technology. Joanne Westwood (Chapter Two) discusses the use of melodrama tactics to portray child trafficking and Anneke Meyer (Chapter Five) highlights how language can be used to construct problems in particular ways. A common thread through these examples is the way that young people, children and childhood are constructed. Childhood is represented as a time of innocence and vulnerability to risk. The discourse of child protection is highly prevalent in relation to both children's use of the internet and child trafficking. Children and young people are represented as passive victims who require protection from dangerous adults. Their vulnerabilities are focused upon at the expense of their strengths. The agency of children and young people is rarely considered in these representations (Cree et al, 2014), denying them a voice regarding their own circumstances and futures.

In Chapter One Ian Butler describes how particular child deaths become scandals that then influence the formation of child-protection policy and practice. Specific child deaths are laden with new meanings as they are chosen by claims makers to advance particular agendas. The phenomenon of child abuse is represented to society by reference to only its most extreme examples, rather than its more prevalent and systemic forms. This distorted emphasis has led to a stereotyping of child abuse that places child abusers as 'others', beyond the moral pale, leading to a neglect of structural and social factors in the aetiology of child abuse. Within a scandal or moral panic the characteristics of the phenomenon, individual or group come to be regarded as symptomatic of something more widespread. This can lead to whole classes or types of people, and often young people, being demonised as 'folk devils', such as Stanley Cohen's (1972) 'Mods and Rockers' and Hall et al's (1978) 'muggers'. In the example of the tragic death of Peter Connelly ('Baby P'), it was the kinds of families who are often the clients of social work that were vilified and used as evidence of the failure of the welfare state, marking an ideological shift in the politics of welfare. This served the particular neoliberal agenda to move responsibility for social problems away from the state and onto individuals and families who could then be held as at fault for the problems they faced, rather than the problems being the consequence of structural or social factors, and thus permitting increasingly punitive approaches to families. Social work and social workers have also at various times been portrayed as a social threat, and failures to protect children have been blamed on the shortcomings of individual social workers rather than on the political or social context in which they operate.

Disproportionate responses and stigmatisation are characteristic of moral panics and create difficulties in understanding more deeply the nature of social problems. Moral panics tend both to be engendered by and to lead to further, disproportionate or inappropriate responses. In Chapter Four Ethel Quayle describes the increase in social control and greater restrictions placed on children using the internet, due to increased anxiety and aversion to risk. Resources are diverted towards control measures and away from researching the protective potential of technology. In relation to child trafficking, there is an emphasis on harm prevention and risk management, tending to increase social control. According to Ian Butler (Chapter One), responses to child welfare scandals have tended to promote the development of a compliance culture within the child-protection system. Social workers become the target of control measures. Many of the changes stemming from inquiries into child deaths have tended to focus on regulation and controlling the workforce, rather than on directly addressing the causes of child abuse. While some improvements in the child-protection system have been made in the past 30 years, much has also been counter-productive, due to the tendency towards over-prescription and bureaucratisation. At the time of writing, the report of the *Independent Inquiry into Child Sexual Exploitation in Rotherham* (Jay, 2014) was released. This is the latest in a series of scandals relating to sexual abuse that have been in the headlines since the exposure of Jimmy Saville as a paedophile. It has prompted renewed calls for a system of mandatory reporting of child abuse, with criminal sanctions (Starmer, 2014; Townsend and Doward, 2014), although in this case it is also asserted that concerns were reported by front-line social workers and youth workers but not subsequently acted upon at a senior level. In such a climate within the UK, an understanding of moral panics is very relevant. This is well illustrated by Anneke Meyer's analysis (Chapter Five) of the media response to the scandal, although she suggests that the idea of moral panic does not necessarily capture all the complexity of specific cases and media reporting is not necessarily homogeneous. Another analysis of this can be seen in a blog by Cree (2014).

Themes from the analyses of moral panics resonate strongly with findings from the Munro (2011) *Review of Child Protection*. This comprehensive review of the child-protection system in England and Wales was requested by the UK government, due to the perceived lack of improvements in the system despite numerous inquiries into child deaths. In the first part of the review (Munro, 2010), it was noted that previous reforms to the child-protection system have led to an 'imbalance and distortion of practice priorities' (Munro, 2010, p 5). Professional practice has become driven by compliance with rules and regulation, rather than based upon professional relationships with children, young people and their families (Munro, 2010, p 8). Child-protection referrals in England and Wales had been on a steadily increasing trend but this had risen sharply following the death of Peter Connelly, suggesting that net-widening was having a significant impact on the child-protection system. According to Munro (2011, pp 134–5), 'The false hope of eliminating risk has contributed significantly to the repeated use of increasing prescription as the solution to perceived problems. Consequently, this has increased defensive practice by professionals so that children and young people's best interests are not always at the heart of decisions.' The problems experienced by children and families that contribute to child-protection concerns are due to multiple and complex factors that cannot be reduced to simplistic or superficial explanations. Munro (2011) states that the combination of a bureaucratised compliance culture and high caseloads has placed pressure on the time that practitioners have to spend with children, building relationships with them, understanding their views and getting to know their families and networks. This has negatively impacted upon the knowledge that practitioners have of the children and families they work with, consequently undermining the quality of assessment and decision making (cf Thomas and Holland, 2010). In an attempt to cope with these pressures, the child-protection system has become focused upon investigation in order to eliminate the likelihood of children's being killed or seriously injured, taking attention and resources away from preventative practice. This has led to what Clapton et al (2013) describe as 'fortress social work', in which there has been a coarsening of attitudes towards families and a deterioration in relationships: the role of social services has become that of monitoring and surveillance rather than the provision of support. It is hardly surprising, in these circumstances, that recruitment and retention of social workers has remained a significant issue when social workers struggle to practise in ways that are congruent with what motivated them to join the profession in the first place (Social Work (Scotland), 2014).

The Munro Review recommends that children should be at the heart of the child-protection system, and promoting the best outcomes for children and young people requires that social workers develop meaningful relationships with them and their families. Professional practice has to be underpinned by sound knowledge of theory and research, and barriers to professional judgement have to be removed. Social work expertise needs to be developed through the creation of learning (rather than compliance) cultures within child-protection work. These recommendations have generally been warmly received by social work practitioners not only in England and Wales but also in the rest of the UK. While there appears to be a willingness within the social work profession to move in the direction that Munro proposed, there are concerns that the impetus for change has been undermined by austerity cuts to public services in the UK. Many consider these cuts themselves to be ideologically driven, in line with Ian Butler's analysis (Chapter One). This leaves the likelihood of positive change uncertain, and the Munro Review may acquire the status of another well-meaning report, unless its recommendations are put into practice (Edmondson et al, 2013).

Moral-panic writings provide a lens through which a significant part of the story of the difficulties currently being faced within child-welfare and child-protection systems can be understood. It provides conceptual tools and analyses that can help to explain some of the macro-level drivers influencing social work policy and practice. The contributions in this byte have highlighted that 'moral panics do harm in the "real" world' (Cree et al, 2014, p 32): they influence the understanding of social problems, the distribution of resources, the way in which individuals and groups of people are treated and the context within which social workers practise and social policy is made. An understanding informed by moral panic perspectives is therefore valuable to practitioners in order to critically reflect on social problems and challenge social injustice (Cree et al, 2014). The concept of moral entrepreneurs or claims makers also provides a useful concept by which social workers can question their own practice and the claims they make regarding the children and families with whom they work. It is not only the media and politicians who can be swept up by moral panics (cf Wastell and White, 2012). As a profession we need, I believe, to ground social work expertise, in terms of knowledge, values and skills, on the relationships we have with children and their families, and not fall into the trap of reductionism and stereotyping to impose a false sense of certainty over the complexity of people's lives: 'The problems with which social work engages are ancient and recalcitrant. Only the most nuanced arguments hold any real promise, yet these are often conspicuous by their absence' (Featherstone et al, 2014, p 53). Social workers need time and discretion to build relationships with children, young people and their families if they are to develop the kind of 'nuanced arguments' required. We also need time to think and learn, and a moral panic perspective can be a valuable conceptual tool for practitioners' reflections on policy and practice.

References

Clapton, G., Cree, V. and Smith, M. (2013) 'Critical commentary: moral panics, claims-making and child protection in the UK', *British Journal of Social Work*, vol 43, no 4, pp 803–12.

Cohen, S. (1972) *Folk devils and moral panics. The creation of the Mods and Rockers*, London: MacGibbon and Kee Ltd.

Cree, V. (2014) 'The Rotherham inquiry – an alternative view', ESRC Moral Panic Seminar Series 2012–2014 (5 October), http://moralpanicseminarseries.wordpress.com/2014/10/05/the-rotherham-inquiry-an-alternative-view/.

Cree, V., Clapton, G. and Smith, M. (2014) 'The presentation of child trafficking in the UK: an old and new moral panic?', *British Journal of Social Work*, vol 44, no 2, pp 418–33.

Edmondson, D., Potter, A. and McLaughlin, H. (2013) 'Reflections of a higher specialist PQ student group on the Munro recommendations for children's social workers', *Practice: Social Work in Action*, vol 25, no 3, pp 191–207.

Featherstone, B., White, S. and Morris, K. (2014) *Re-imagining child protection*, Bristol: Policy Press.

Hall, S., Critcher, C., Jefferson, T., Clarke, J. and Roberts, B. (1978) *Policing the crisis. Mugging, the state and law and order*, London: Macmillan.

Hothersall, S. (2014) *Social work with children, young people and their families in Scotland* (3rd edn), London: Sage.

Jay, A. (2014) *Independent inquiry into child sexual exploitation in Rotherham (1997–2013)*, www.rotherham.gov.uk/inquiry (accessed 27 August 2014).

Lonne, B., Parton, N., Thomson, J. and Harries, M. (2009) *Reforming child protection*, Abingdon: Routledge.

Munro, E. (2010) *The Munro Review of Child Protection Part One: A systems analysis*, London: Department of Education.

Munro, E. (2011) *The Munro Review of Child Protection Final Report: A child-centred system*, London: Department of Education.

Social Work (Scotland) (2014) 'Massive rise in vacant posts in England – but what's the cause?', *Professional Social Work*, September, p 8.

Starmer, K. (2014) 'How can we prevent another Rotherham?', *Guardian* (28 August), www.theguardian.com/commentisfree/2014/aug/28/how-can-we-prevent-another-rotherham.

Thomas, J. and Holland, S. (2010) 'Representing children's identities in core assessments', *British Journal of Social Work*, vol 40, pp 2617–33.

Townsend, M. and Doward, J. (2014) 'Rotherham: Yvette Cooper calls for change of law after abuse scandal', *Observer* (30 August), www.theguardian.com/uk-news/2014/aug/30/rotherham-yvette-cooper-call-law-change.

Wastell, D. and White, S. (2012) 'Blinded by neuroscience: social policy, the family and the infant brain', *Families, Relationships and Society*, vol 1, no 3, pp 397–414.